"Most books on the cross of Christ are regurgitations of outmoded atonement theories that say almost nothing memorable. But Brian Zahnd has once again broken the mold with his revolutionary book *The Wood Between the Worlds*. Herein we have a capacious portrait of Jesus' sacrifice that is so stunningly beautiful and uniquely framed that the reader cannot look away. An enrapturing volume to reignite the church's curiosity around the crucifixion penned by one of today's most provocative pastors."

Jonathan Merritt, author and contributing writer for *The Atlantic*

"To the apostolic witnesses, the cross of Christ was never a theory to be solved by theologizing, as if the calculative mind could solve its mysteries through abstraction. The cross can only be narrated, beheld, and shared as a transforming testimony—proclaimed in sermons, symbols, and parables, in the poetry and hymns of lives it has rebirthed. For over four decades, Brian Zahnd has been a poet-preacher-prophet of the cross. I daresay he's an eyewitness theologian who kneels at its foot. This book is his revelation of who he has seen there."

Bradley Jersak, principal of St. Stephen's University, New Brunswick, and author of *A More Christlike Word*

"With the heart of a pastor, the mind of a scholar, and the soul of a Jesus follower, Brian Zahnd here shares the fruit of his long, unhurried contemplation of the cross of Christ. His keen insights liberate us from flawed atonement theories based in retributive justice that have persisted for far too long, and he breathes new life into the mystery of the cross: the supreme centerpiece of God's love that radiates redemption and ushers us into the peaceable kingdom."

Eric E. Peterson, pastor of Colbert Presbyterian Church

"The American church has inherited a desiccated theology of the cross, one that bypasses the rich and diverse images of salvation presented in Scripture and articulates atonement in terms of deity appeasement and individualistic salvation. In *The Wood Between the Worlds*, Brian Zahnd puts flesh back on the dry bones of our atonement theology. His holistic reading of the biblical texts recounts the salvation story with an eye toward what the cross meant and continues to mean for the world. Using literary allusions, Girard's scapegoat theory, and reflections on our current social and political reality, Zahnd refocuses us on the truth of the gospel message—that Jesus' death saves humanity not from hands of an angry God but from the violent powers that have corrupted us and held us in their sway. The efficacy of the cross, then, is not that it divides the damned from the saved but that it unites all humanity, reconciling us to one another in hope as we hunger for the final restoration of creation."

Jennifer Garcia Bashaw, associate professor of New Testament and Christian ministry at Campbell University

THE WOOD
BETWEEN
THE WORLDS

A POETIC THEOLOGY
OF THE CROSS

BRIAN ZAHND

An imprint of InterVarsity Press
Downers Grove, Illinois

InterVarsity Press
P.O. Box 1400 | Downers Grove, IL 60515-1426
ivpress.com | email@ivpress.com

InterVarsity Press® is the publishing division of InterVarsity Christian Fellowship/USA®. For more information, visit intervarsity.org.

Published in association with The Bindery Agency, www.TheBinderyAgency.com.

While any stories in this book are true, some names and identifying information may have been changed to protect the privacy of individuals.

The publisher cannot verify the accuracy or functionality of website URLs used in this book beyond the date of publication.

Cover design: David Fassett
Interior design: Jeanna Wiggins
Cover images: © Javier Zayas Photography / Getty Images; © Jay's photo / Getty Images;
        The Crucifixion by Andreas Pavias / National Gallery of Athens / Wikimedia Commons

ISBN 978-1-5140-0562-0 (print) | ISBN 978-1-5140-0563-7 (digital)

Printed in the United States of America ♾

Library of Congress Cataloging-in-Publication Data
Names: Zahnd, Brian, author.
Title: The wood between the worlds : a poetic theology of the cross / Brian
  Zahnd.
Description: Downers Grove, IL : InterVarsity Press, [2024] | Includes
  bibliographical references.
Identifiers: LCCN 2023021195 (print) | LCCN 2023021196 (ebook) | ISBN
  9781514005620 (print) | ISBN 9781514005637 (digital)
Subjects: LCSH: Holy Cross. | God (Christianity) | Jesus
  Christ–Crucifixion. | Theology of the cross. | Phenomenological
  theology.
Classification: LCC BT453 .Z34 2024 (print) | LCC BT453 (ebook) | DDC
  232.96/3–dc23/eng/20230731
LC record available at https://lccn.loc.gov/2023021195
LC ebook record available at https://lccn.loc.gov/2023021196

FOR THE SQUAD

CONTENTS

PRELUDE

I DARE TO WRITE ABOUT GOD, which is, admittedly, an audacious undertaking. That a bit of sentient soil would venture to say something about the nature of the ineffable eternal must seem like the most absurd of fool's errands. And yet I venture. I cannot help myself. The depth of my fascination with the One who is the answer to the question of why there is something instead of nothing makes it impossible for me to remain silent on the subject. I sympathize with King David when he said, "While I mused, the fire burned; then I spoke with my tongue" (Ps 39:3). And when I dare to speak about God, I do so not as the idly curious but as a reverent worshiper. I seek to understand God not as a cold and dispassionate scientist—a Godologist, if you will—but as one who prays, worships, and kneels before his maker.

In seeking to understand God, I am not starting from square one—far from it. Theologically, I am not tasked with harnessing fire or inventing the wheel. I am the heir of a venerable theological tradition, among the grateful recipients of received revelation that has been passed down for millennia. I am working from the sacred text that is the Jewish and Christian Scriptures. In daring to write about God I do so with the language given to us in the Bible. I can truthfully say that my thinking is saturated in Scripture—the Bible is my primary vocabulary. Yet as essential as Scripture is, to say that the Bible clearly reveals the nature of God is to oversimplify the matter.

The Bible is a sprawling collection of texts often unwieldy and difficult to interpret. While some may speak glibly of the alleged perspicuity of Scripture, we nevertheless must acknowledge the uncomfortable reality of what Christian Smith has called "pervasive interpretive pluralism."[1] In other words, no matter how ardently we hold to the inspiration of Scripture and insist on its clarity, the text must be interpreted, and there is no denying we are far from universal agreement on biblical interpretation. Thus it behooves us to approach the task of theological interpretation with a good deal of humility.

In seeking to interpret the biblical text with a goal of gaining insight into the nature of God, we need a way of positioning ourselves within Scripture. We need to locate an interpretive center—a focal point from which we can interpret the rest of the Bible. We need to locate the heart of the Bible. As a Christian, I have a ready and, what seems to me, obvious location for the heart of the Bible: the cross. In the Christian gospel, everything leads to the cross and proceeds from it.

If the Bible is ultimately the grand saga of human redemption through divine intervention, the crucifixion of Jesus Christ is *literally* the crux of the story. The cross is the axis upon which the biblical story turns. Who is God? God is the one who was crucified between two criminals on Good Friday. Hints at the nature of God are subsumed into a full unveiling of the divine nature at Golgotha. On Good Friday the true nature of God is on full display in Jesus of Nazareth crucified. God is the crucified one. And yet, nothing is more central to the theological vocation than interpreting the meaning of God as revealed in the crucified Christ. Theologians must gather worshipfully around the cross of Christ and speak from there. All that can truthfully be said about God is somehow present at the cross.

Yet I suspect that what can be said about God revealed in the crucified Christ is as infinite as God's own being. Though we can begin talking about the meaning of the cross, we can never conclude the conversation. The four living creatures around the throne of God who day and night sing, "Holy, holy, holy, / the Lord God the Almighty, / who was and is and is to come" (Rev 4:8), are not automatons on infinite repeat, but angels granted an infinite series of glimpses into the ever-unfolding glory of God. Every eruption of their thrice-holy adoration is a reflexive response to a new glimpse of God's glory. How the seraphim gather around the throne of God is how theologians should gather around the cross of Christ.

The meaning of the cross is not singular, but kaleidoscopic. Each turn of a kaleidoscope reveals a new geometric image. This is how we must approach our interpretation of the cross—through the eyepiece of a theological kaleidoscope. That the word *kaleidoscope* is a Greek word meaning "beautiful form" makes this all the more apropos. I believe it is safe to assume there are an infinite number of ways of viewing the cross of Christ as the beautiful form that saves the world. In this book I seek to share some of the beautiful forms I see as I gaze upon the cross through my theological kaleidoscope.

Then there is the matter of how to speak of what is seen through the theological kaleidoscope. Not all theological language is the same. Though in modernity we have a penchant for technical prose when engaging in theological conversation, earlier ages—and the Bible itself—have a fondness for the less precise but also less limiting language of poetry. Theopoetics is, in part, an attempt to speak of the divine in more poetic language. It is an attempt to rise above the dull and prosaic world of matter-of-fact dogma that tends to shut down further conversation. If in this book I occasionally veer away from prose to employ slightly more poetic language in how I see the cross, this should not be regarded as fanciful, but as the best recourse I could find to describe the truth I believe the Spirit is helping me to see. It's an invitation to consider something new. With that, let us begin what I hope will be a kaleidoscopic and theopoetic conversation about the wood between the worlds.

Advent 2022

1

THE WOOD BETWEEN
THE WORLDS

There's blood on the wood between the worlds.

BOB AYALA

WHEN WE LOOK AT A CRUCIFIX what do we see? A naked man
nailed to a tree. A macabre image of bleeding flesh fastened to wood
by cold iron. Viewed objectively it's abhorrent—like those ghastly
photos of lynchings. Strangely, many find solace as they look upon a
depiction of this naked man nailed to a tree. Finding comfort in such
death is a mystery we will explore. But most modern people find it
neither ghastly nor consoling—for them it's just a banal religious
cliché barely noticed. On canvas and wood, in stone and metal, the
crucifixion of Jesus Christ has been painted, carved, sculpted, and
molded billions of times. *Billions!* Everyone has seen a crucifix. Its
long history and sheer ubiquity have rendered it almost invisible. Yet
if we give just a moment of serious consideration to a crucifix it is
still capable of shocking us, if for no other reason than it is such an
outrageous anthropological absurdity.

From our beginning, we Homo sapiens have created images as a
way of representing and interpreting our world. We took up painting
while living in caves. Those located in Cáceres, Spain, are sixty-four

thousand years old! We've been doing this for a long time. Clearly, we are a species given to symbolic artistic endeavor. It's not tangential to our being—it's central. Whether in primitive cave paintings or masterpieces housed in museums, we have sought to depict through art that which gives meaning to our lives. Art is a window into the human imagination.

Now reflect upon this strange fact: our single most depicted story-image is of a man nailed to a tree. Considered from an anthropological point of view, how bizarre it is that Jesus of Nazareth portrayed as crucified is the most replicated work of art in human history! This must indicate something deeply significant about the human experience. Of course religion is at work here. Christians bring meaning to the crucifixion by confessing that the crucified one is, in fact, God. Nevertheless, the religious element doesn't explain everything. Depictions of deities and their avatars have been common throughout history, be it Ra shining like the sun, Krishna riding triumphantly in his chariot, or Buddha sitting in the tranquil bliss of enlightenment. But the depiction of a tortured god nailed to a tree is not something we would expect. A crucified god is an absurd incongruity, yet it's the event we have depicted the most. *That* must mean something!

Ask yourself this question: What would alien visitors to our planet make of our billions of crucifixes? I once saw a cartoon that illustrates this point. Two space aliens who have just landed their flying saucer on Earth are standing in front of a life-sized crucifix, like the kind you can find along roadsides in Spain. One alien says to the other, "You know what we need to do? We need to get the f— out of here, that's what we need to do." The expletive accentuates the absurdist humor. The cartoon may be somewhat profane, but it also alerts us to how shocking and unsettling a crucifix is when considered objectively. The aliens have concluded that a planet whose inhabitants erect public depictions of crucifixions is probably not a safe place—and they are not wrong.

The space alien cartoon is not the first to use the crucifixion as its subject matter. Around AD 200 someone scratched a blasphemous

graffiti on a plaster wall in Rome, evidently intended to mock a
Christian by the name of Alexamenos. It depicts a crucified man with
the head of a donkey, while a young man worships the crucified victim.
An inscription in misspelled Greek reads, "Alexamenos worships his
god." (Note that this image, as well as several other pieces of art that are
referenced, can be viewed on the color insert near the center of this book.)

Clearly someone thought it comical that Alexamenos worshiped
the god of the Christians—a Galilean Jew who had been crucified by
the Roman governor Pontius Pilate. What did Alexamenos think of
this insult? We may know. In a room adjacent to where the blas-
phemous graffiti was found, another graffiti written in another hand
reads, "Alexamenos is faithful." This is a fascinating glimpse into the
world of early Christianity—a time long before the worship of a
crucified god could be dismissed as cliché.

A Camino of Crucifixes

My wife and I have walked the five-hundred-mile Francés route on the
Camino de Santiago across northern Spain numerous times, but our
first trek began (by happy accident) on Holy Cross Day, September 14.
On this feast day dedicated to the cross itself, I sensed the Holy Spirit
giving me some specific instructions for our forty-day pilgrimage:

Enter every church you can.

Pay attention to the crucifix.

Ask what does this mean?

Don't be too quick to give an answer.

For forty days and five hundred miles I paid attention to hundreds
of crucifixes, always asking what it meant and resisting easy answers.
It was a profound spiritual exercise.

In the Protestant world crucifixes are uncommon, and in many
denominations, they are altogether absent. Instead of portraying
Christ as crucified, many Protestant churches have opted for an ab-
stract symbol of a cross. Ostensibly it represents the same thing, but
absent a crucified Christ it is easy to sanitize the cross to a prosaic

theological formula. A geometric design of two interesting lines does not evoke the pathos of a crucifix. Geometry doesn't tell a story.

As a Protestant I had not been around the life-sized crucifixes found in Catholic churches on a regular basis, but now I was encountering them several times a day. Contemplating them was a powerful reminder that the crucifixion of Jesus Christ was not an equation in a salvation formula; it was an *event*. It was something that happened within history. Because I was on pilgrimage, I wasn't seeing the same crucifix over and over. Instead, I saw hundreds of different crucifixes, but they were not mass-produced copies. Each crucifix, whether in a grand cathedral or in a small village chapel, was an original. In some Jesus was serene, in others he was in anguish. In some Jesus was still alive, in others he had already died. Some were strangely beautiful, while others accentuated the horror. One of my favorites stood in a tiny hilltop chapel near Zabaldika, surrounded by hundreds of green Post-it notes, giving it the appearance of Jesus crucified in a verdant forest. Upon closer inspection the notes were prayer requests written by pilgrims. The crucified Christ in a forest of prayer was an exceptionally peaceful place.

For six weeks I saw different crucifixes every day, and as I walked, I meditated on what it meant that when the Son of God came into the world he was nailed to a tree. I heeded the Spirit's admonition to resist a quick answer. This is the bane of tidy atonement theories. The idea that we can sum up the meaning of the crucifixion in a sentence or two borders on the blasphemous. Atonement theories have an unfortunate tendency to reduce the crucifixion to a single meaning. This is an enormous mistake. If you're going to dabble in atonement theories, at least keep it plural. Reducing the cross to a single meaning quarantines the cross so it doesn't touch too many areas of our lives.

The crucifixion means everything. Everything that can be known about God is in some way present at the cross.

It's the pinnacle of divine self-disclosure, the eternal moment of forgiveness, divine solidarity with human suffering, the enduring model of discipleship, the supreme demonstration of divine love, the beauty that saves the world, the re-founding of the world around an axis of love, the overthrow of the satan, the shaming of the principalities and powers, the unmasking of mob violence, the condemnation of state violence, the exposé of political power, the abolition of war, the sacrifice to end sacrificing, the great divide of humankind, the healing center of the cosmos, the death by which death is conquered, the Lamb upon the throne, the tree of life recovered and revealed. And with this brief list of interpretations, I've come nowhere near exhausting the meaning of the cross, for indeed the crucifixion of Jesus Christ is an inexhaustible revelation of who God is.

This book is my humble attempt to communicate some of the mysteries I've glimpsed while meditating on Christ crucified. I've written all my books with a candle burning in front of a Byzantine cross icon sitting on my writing desk. I want Christ crucified to preside over every book I write, but especially this one. I won't try to "sum up" what the cross means, as doing so would be to treat the cross dismissively. Instead, I want to muse on the deep mystery of the cross. Rather than searching for a final word, I seek an eternal recurrence of holy awe.

I want to be drawn into a contemplative orbit around the cross. Because along with everything else the cross is, it is the epicenter of Christian faith. At the center of the gospel we don't find perennial wisdom spirituality, proverbial advice on how to achieve success, or "practical sermons" that you can "apply to your life." What we find is the disorienting story of the God-Man nailed to a tree. *Christ crucified is ever and always the true focus of the gospel proclamation.*

This is why the apostle Paul told the Corinthians that in proclaiming the mystery of God, he determined to know nothing except Jesus Christ and him crucified (1 Cor 2:2). As we look at the cross, we encounter the mystery of God, not an atonement theory. I don't want to reduce the cross to one of the Four Spiritual Laws or a waypoint on the Roman Road or a single sentence in a statement of faith. We don't need a technical manual on the cross, we need something more like a theopoetics of the cross.

The cross of Christ is the wood between the worlds.
There is the world that was and the world to come,
and in between those two worlds
is the wood upon which the Son of God was hung.

A Tale of Two Trees

Trees abound at the beginning of the Bible. At the center of our paradisiacal innocence that was Eden, there were two mysterious trees— the tree of life and the tree of the knowledge of good and evil. Both trees were blessed by God, but the fruit of the second tree eaten out of season was poisonous. And that's when the trouble began. Loss of innocence, shame and blame, banishment and exile followed. Adam and Eve were forced to venture into a world bereft of the tree of life. Outside the gates of Eden the specter of death awaited them. The first death did not come from Adam or Eve having grown old, but when their firstborn slew their second son. (Was it with a wooden club fashioned from a tree as Pietro Novelli depicts in a famous painting?)

After his crime Cain fled east of Eden to found the first city. And the blood of all the slain Abels throughout history cries against the violence that is the foundation of human civilization. We live in the world that war hath wrought. Cain inaugurated the pattern that all great empires would follow, what the Bible cryptically calls Babylon. Cain's fratricidal DNA is found in the genetics of every empire: Call your brother other and enemy. Tell yourself it must be done. Slay the indigenous Abels. Hide the bodies. Lie to yourself and God about it. Move further away from Eden. Repeat, repeat, repeat . . .

This is the world that was, and in many ways still is. But in the midst of history something has happened. The tree of life has been found again. This eternal tree was first planted by God in paradise and then lost to the sons of Adam and daughters of Eve when the gates of Eden closed behind them. But this time, the tree of life was not planted in paradise; it was planted upon a skull-like hill called Golgotha. It's a forlorn tree having but two branches. It was, in fact, a killing tree. Its strange and bitter fruit was death for all who hung upon it. Golgotha's tree embraced living men and released them only once they were dead.

This was the tree upon which the living One was hung. Jesus of Nazareth. The Christ. The Son of Man. The Son of God. The Lamb of God. The Word of God. The Logos made flesh. The New Adam. The way, the truth, and the life. Crucifixion can extinguish the life of those who are already dead in their sins and trespasses, but this is no mere son of Adam; this is the Son of the living God. "'The first man, Adam, became a living being'; the last Adam became a life-giving spirit" (1 Cor 15:45). The Son of God entered the world of the dead and dying children of Adam as one possessing the spirit of life—and "the life of the flesh is in the blood" (Lev 17:11). When the blood of the Son of God stained the wood that stood upon Skull Hill, it became the tree of life. What once was lost behind the closed gates of Eden has now been found. The cross of Christ *is* the tree of life. Our long exile east of Eden is over and we can at last return home. The tree of life has forever opened the once-closed gates of paradise (Rev 2:7; 21:25; 22:14).

The cross of Christ is the wood between the worlds—the world that was and the world to come.

At the end of the Nicene Creed, Christians confess, "we look for the resurrection of the dead, and the life of the world to come." According to our great confession there is a world to come—a world whose eschatological vision is set forth at the end of the Bible with these exceedingly hopeful words:

See, the home of God is among mortals.
He will dwell with them;
they will be his peoples,
and God himself will be with them and be their God;

he will wipe every tear from their eyes.

Death will be no more;

mourning and crying and pain will be no more,

for the first things have passed away. (Rev 21:3-4)

Christians confess that the world to come is somehow made possible by the cross of Christ. As in C. S. Lewis's Chronicles of Narnia, the wood between the worlds is a portal. In this world of sin and death we do not despair because we believe the cross will transport us to a world where, in the beloved words of Lady Julian, "All will be well, and all will be well, and all manner of things will be well."[1]

Space aliens looking at a crucifix may see nothing but a graphic testament to a violent world, but we who believe the gospel story see something else. We see the place where an old world died with the death of Christ, and we see the act of redemption that opened the door to a world made new. Mel Gibson's *Passion of the Christ* had its flaws, but anachronistically placing "See, I am making all things new" (Rev 21:5) in the mouth of Jesus as he carries his cross to Golgotha was a sophisticated artistic and theological move. The cross really is the point from which the world is made new. And though we still await the full arrival of the new Jerusalem, those in Christ inhabit the liminal space of the now and not yet. Clearly, we are still part of the old world that is passing away, but we also belong, even now, to the new creation to come.

Saint Paul says it like this: "So if anyone is in Christ, there is a new creation: everything old has passed away; look, new things have come into being" (2 Cor 5:17). From the vantage of the wood between the worlds we see both realities at the same time. We see the broken world that everyone else sees, but we also catch glimpses of the beautiful world to come. Inspired by what we see in the world to come, we advocate for its possibility here and now. This is part of the prophetic task of the church. In his book *Reality, Grief, Hope*, Walter Brueggemann says the three prophetic tasks of the church are to tell the truth in a society that lives in illusion, grieve in a society that practices denial, and express hope in a society that lives in despair.[2] And the cross is always the primary source for the church's prophetic witness.

THE SCANDAL OF THE CROSS

If we encountered the aliens before they fled in their flying saucer and attempted some extraterrestrial evangelism by explaining that the crucifix is a retelling of what happened to God when he visited our planet, but that his crucifixion was, in fact, the act which saves the world . . . well, I can imagine some alien incredulity. But perhaps no more than what the apostles encountered in the Greco-Roman world of late antiquity. The apostle Paul readily admitted that for his Jewish audience the message of a crucified messiah was an outrageous scandal, while his Gentile audience found the very notion of a crucified god laughable and foolish (1 Cor 1:23).

The gospel is not sensible advice on how to have a better life. If what Paul and subsequent Christians claim about the cross is not true, it is either a scandalous blasphemy or a ludicrous joke. Put bluntly, the cross *is* an offence. Its meaning is not clear to either religious expectations or common sense. If in the time of the apostles you were trying to invent a religion with mass appeal, you wouldn't place a crucifixion at the center of it. A sacrificial or heroic death, perhaps, but not a *crucifixion*.

At the dawn of Christianity, crucifixion was so repulsive that the word itself was avoided in polite company. Fleming Rutledge observes, "The cross is by a very long way the most *irreligious* object ever to find its way into the heart of faith."[3] Midway through the first century AD, who could have predicted that within a few hundred years there would be millions of people who believed that a *crucified* Jew from Galilee is indeed the Son of God and Savior of the world? Yet this is exactly what happened. Significantly, the apostles and first evangelists didn't try to *prove* the gospel of the cross; they *proclaimed* it. Their gospel message wasn't an analytic explanation; it was a shocking announcement. They proclaimed a message that had at its center what contemporary society considered the vilest concept imaginable: crucifixion. And as improbable as it seems, this message eventually turned the Roman world upside down and altered the course of Western civilization.

How do we explain this? In a word, resurrection. The Romans crucified hundreds of thousands of people, most of them slaves and rebels. Crucifixion was horrific but not uncommon. From the point of view of those who passed by Golgotha on Good Friday, there was nothing unique in the crucifixion of the Galilean who hung in the center of three crosses. What is unique is Easter. Christ the crucified is also Christ the risen. When we speak of the crucifixion of Jesus Christ it is always in light of the resurrection. It is the light shining from the empty tomb that illuminates the cross so that we can understand it correctly. When we speak of the crucified Christ, we always mean the crucified-risen Christ. To properly interpret the crucifixion and the resurrection they must always be held together. What Saint Peter said to the Sanhedrin is the foundation for understanding the cross: "The God of our ancestors raised up Jesus, whom you had killed by hanging him on a tree" (Acts 5:30). The tree of Calvary is the wood between the old world dominated by death and the new world animated by resurrection. And it's in this light that we can begin to explore what it all means.

2

THE SINGULARITY
OF GOOD FRIDAY

Terrible fruit was on the tree
In the acre of Gethsemane;
For us by Calvary's distress
The wine was racked from the press;
Now in our altar-vessels stored
Is the sweet Vintage of our Lord.

GERARD MANLEY HOPKINS, "BARNFLOOR AND WINEPRESS"

MOST OF US INSTINCTIVELY ASSOCIATE Good Friday with the forgiveness of sins, and that instinct is correct.[1] Something happened on Good Friday that makes the forgiveness of all sins possible. But how does this forgiveness work? Saint Paul says, "Christ died for our sins in accordance with the scriptures" (1 Cor 15:3). But what does that mean? Did Christ's death somehow restore honor to an insulted omnipotent monarch as some have suggested? Is the crucifixion a ghastly appeasement of an offended deity through the torture and execution of an innocent victim? On Good Friday did God vent his anger by brutally killing his Son so he could finally find the wherewithal to forgive? Are we to imagine that John 3:16 actually means God so *hated* the world that he *killed* his only begotten Son? No, imposing the primitive notion of a sacrificial appeasement upon the cross is what N. T. Wright describes as "the paganizing of atonement theology."[2]

If we construe an idea that atonement means the appeasement of God's anger through the violent abuse of his Son, we have viewed the cross through a pagan lens. The events of Good Friday are not God punishing his Son. Wright explains,

> If we arrive at that conclusion, we know that we have not just made a trivial mistake that could be easily corrected, but a major blunder. We have portrayed God not as the generous Creator, the loving Father, but as an angry despot. That idea belongs not to the biblical picture of God, but with pagan beliefs.[3]

The cross is not what God *inflicts* in order to forgive; the cross is what God in Christ *endures* as he forgives. This is an essential and enormous clarification! At the cross the Son does not act as an agent of change upon the Father. Orthodox theology has always insisted that God is not subject to change or mutation. Rather, God is immutable. Thus the cross is not where Jesus *changes* God but where Jesus *reveals* God. On Good Friday Jesus does not save us from God; Jesus reveals God as Savior! We don't have to imagine the Son pacifying an angry Father in order to understand Good Friday as the epicenter of forgiveness.

But if the point is not appeasement, how *do* we associate Good Friday with forgiveness? Allow me to suggest that we think about it like this: *On Good Friday the sin of the world coalesced into a hideous singularity that upon the cross it might be forgiven en masse.*

THE EPICENTER OF HISTORY

The cross really is the wood between the worlds because it is the true center of history. Everything leads up to and flows from the cross. The death of God upon a tree is not just some event within history, but *the* event that defines and explains, reveals and redeems all of history. However we understand the origin of sin within the human story, its trajectory moves inevitably toward Good Friday. And however we understand the salvation of the world, the task given by the Father to the Son, it all flows forth from the eternal moment within time when Jesus, nailed to the wood between the worlds, prayed, "Father, forgive them, for they do not know what they are doing" (Lk 23:34). From that moment both our primordial past and our most distant future fall under the redeeming work of grace.

The "Father, forgive them" moment upon the cross is not when Jesus changed the mercurial mind of God. No! This is the moment when the eternal love of the triune God intervened decisively in human history to forgive human sin once and for all. This is the moment when the Spirit of love that flows between the Father and the Son erupted to engulf and forgive the sin of the world. The prophet Zechariah imagined it with this prophecy: "On that day a fountain shall be opened . . . to cleanse them from sin" (Zech 13:1). John the Baptist foreshadowed it when he exclaimed, "Behold, the Lamb of God, who takes away the sin of the world" (Jn 1:29 ESV). Paul summed it up like this: "For God was in Christ, reconciling the world to himself, no longer counting people's sins against them" (2 Cor 5:19 NLT).

We can think of Good Friday as the moment in history when the sins of the world became a hideous singularity. On Good Friday all the many sins of the world amalgamated into a single sin—"the sin of the world," as John the Baptist called it. On Good Friday the mystery of iniquity was present in the taunts and jeers, the scourging and crucifixion of the Son of God. As the sun darkened over Golgotha the unspeakable potential of evil became the single sin of deicide, the murder of God. Every sin, from the original Adamic transgression to the final iniquity of a fallen age, became the one sin of killing Jesus. And what happened? Were twelve legions of avenging angels unleashed to wreak divine retribution? Did a thunderclap of damning judgment fall upon the guilty? Did the angel of death appear to slay the executioners of Christ? No, Jesus simply absorbed it all and forgave it all.

Jesus was killed, not by God, but by the hands of wicked men. With great violence the principalities and powers sinned the sin of the world into the sinless body of Jesus. When the sins of the world became the sinful singularity of Good Friday, the one who knew no sin was made to be sin (2 Cor 5:21). The body of Jesus hanging upon the cross was made to be the repository for the sin of the world. What does sin look like? Sin looks like the grotesquely distorted and anguish-ridden body of Christ as depicted by Matthias Grünewald in the *Isenheim Altarpiece*. It looks like the innocent one nailed to a tree bearing in his hands and feet and side the entrance wounds of sin.

But once sin entered the body of the crucified God, there could be no escape. On Good Friday the sin of the world was drawn into the infinite gravity of God's grace. At Golgotha the sin of the world as a hideous singularity was drawn inescapably into the greater singularity of God's love where sin itself was undone. Christ's self-sacrificial death upon the cross became a cosmic supernova irradiating time and space with divine forgiveness. This was when the sin of the world was taken away, as foretold by the forerunner. When Jesus prayed, "Father, forgive them," what was forgiven? Everything. Not only the betrayal committed by Judas; not only the murder committed by Barabbas; not only the false accusations leveled by Caiaphas; not only the unjust sentence handed down by Pontius Pilate; not only the Roman soldiers who crucified Jesus; not only the jeering crowd who mocked Jesus, but *everything*! Every sin, every transgression, every act of idolatry, every deed of injustice, every stone-age murder, every space-age iniquity, every notorious crime, every hidden sin—it was *all* forgiven. On Good Friday all the sins of the world became a single sin that it might be forgiven once and forever. This is what makes Good Friday good!

THE PASSOVER LAMB

Another way we speak of forgiveness in connection with the cross is to speak of the blood of the lamb. Throughout the New Testament the blood of Jesus is connected with salvation. Jesus himself spoke of his blood as a covenant of *forgiveness* (Mt 26:28). Paul says we are *justified* by the blood of Jesus (Rom 5:9). The writer of Hebrews says we are *sanctified* through the blood of Jesus (Heb 13:12). Peter says we are *redeemed* by the blood of Jesus (1 Pet 1:18-19 NIV). John the Revelator says we are *freed* by the blood of Jesus (Rev 1:5).

All this language of covenant, redemption, and freedom through the blood of Jesus as the Lamb of God reaches back to Exodus and the story of the Passover lamb. In Exodus 12 Moses instructed Israel in how to prepare for the tenth and final plague that would come upon Egypt—the plague that would result in their liberation. Each household was to take a yearling male lamb without blemish, keep it in their house for four days, and then at twilight on the fourteenth of Nisan the lamb was to be slain. The flesh of the lamb was roasted to provide the Israelites with the covenant meal of Passover. The blood of the lamb was applied to their doorpost and lintel as a sign that this household was under the protection of God and marked for liberation. "The blood shall be a sign for you on the houses where you live: when I see the blood, I will pass over you, and no plague shall destroy you" (Ex 12:13).

It's important to recognize that the Passover lamb was *not* being punished. Rather, it was a sacrifice to provide the covenant meal. The ritual killing of a human or animal to appease the gods is a pagan practice and not what was observed by the ancient Hebrews in the Exodus story. Hebrew sacrifice was about covenant and union with God (Gen 15), not the placation of a retributive deity. The yearling lamb was not being punished; it was providing a meal as the gathering place for a covenant community. The annual remembrance of the covenant meal and Israel's liberation from bondage in Egypt became the Jewish Passover.

The Passover is what Jesus reimagines on the night of the Last Supper as he describes his flesh and blood as the sacramental meal for a new covenant. This becomes the Christian Eucharist. When we eat the bread and drink the cup of the Lord's Supper, we are saying that we are liberated from our bondage to sin and death through the covenant established in the broken body and shed blood of Jesus Christ—our Passover Lamb. The new covenant meal of the Last Supper was a radical expansion of the original Passover. What was *particular* in the ancient Passover marking Israel as God's chosen people expands to the *universal* at the Last Supper. In the sacrificial death of Christ, the invitation to dine at God's table and be liberated from the universal curse of death is offered to the whole world.

The prophet Isaiah first anticipated this seven centuries before Christ when he described Mount Zion as the place where God would turn a funeral into a feast. The poet tells us that a burial shroud has been cast over all peoples and that a sheet has been pulled over the corpse of all nations. This is the pharaonic tyranny of death that threatens to make life meaningless. But in a stunning act of prophetic imagination Isaiah speaks of a day when Yahweh will act and turn the burial shroud into a tablecloth for the great feast of God. The funeral bier is to be transformed into a banqueting table laden with the finest food and wine. The funeral for all nations is to become a feast of liberation for all peoples! Pay attention to the universal scope of salvation set forth in Isaiah's poem.

> On this mountain the LORD of hosts will make for *all* peoples
>   a feast of rich food, a feast of well-aged wines,
>   of rich food filled with marrow, of well-aged wines
>   strained clear.
> And he will destroy on this mountain
>   the shroud that is cast over *all* peoples,
>   the sheet that is spread over *all* nations;
>   he will swallow up death forever.

Then the Lord GOD will wipe away the tears from *all* faces,
and the disgrace of his people he will take away from *all*
the earth,
for the LORD has spoken.
It will be said on that day,
"See, this is our God; we have waited for him, so that he
might save us.
This is the LORD for whom we have waited;
let us be glad and rejoice in his salvation." (Is 25:6-9,
emphasis added)

On the eve of his suffering, at the Passover meal in the upper room
on Mount Zion, the mountain spoken of by Isaiah, Jesus identified
the rich feast and the fine wine that will liberate the world from its
bondage to death as his own body and blood.

While they were eating, Jesus took a loaf of bread, and after
blessing it he broke it, gave it to the disciples, and said, "Take,
eat; this is my body." Then he took a cup, and after giving
thanks he gave it to them, saying, "Drink from it, all of you; this
is my blood of the covenant, which is poured out for many for
the forgiveness of sins." (Mt 26:26-28)

The blood of the Lamb is the blood of the covenant that lib-
erates the whole world from its bondage to death. The blood of
the Lamb is a ransom paid not to God, but to death. Through the
blood of the Lamb we are ransomed for God. Just as Israel was
ransomed for God from Egypt, now humanity is ransomed for
God from death. This is the theme of the song of the Lamb sung
by the redeemed:

You are worthy to take the scroll
and to break its seals,
for you were slaughtered and by your blood you ransomed
for God

saints from every tribe and language and people and
nation. (Rev 5:9)

THE BLOOD THAT SPEAKS A BETTER WORD

Throughout the New Testament we find a plethora of passages con-
necting the blood of Jesus with the Passover and the exodus, indicating
that we should see Good Friday as the intervening act of God that
rescues humanity from its enslavement to sin and death. But the un-
known writer of the epistle to the Hebrews reaches even further back
than Exodus to provide an interpretive meaning for the shed blood of
Jesus. In a passage emphasizing the superiority of the new covenant as
compared to the Sinai covenant, the writer says, "[You have come] to
Jesus, the mediator of a new covenant, and to the sprinkled blood that
speaks a better word than the blood of Abel" (Heb 12:24).

Cain and Abel were the first two children born to a man called
Humankind (Adam) and a woman called Living (Eve) after their
exile from Eden. What unfolds is the familiar tragedy of a sibling
rivalry that leads to fratricide—a story echoed with Romulus and
Remus in the founding myth of Rome, and with Sméagol and Déagol
in *The Lord of the Rings*. Cain was a tiller of the ground; Abel was a
keeper of sheep. An archetypal farmer and shepherd who will come
into competition. Anthropologists tell us violent conflicts regularly
occurred between the farmers who first harnessed agriculture and
the nomadic herdsmen following their flocks during the initial rise
of complex civilization in Mesopotamia. The source of their conflict
was over the use of land. Was land something that could not be pos-
sessed, as the ancient nomads thought, or could it now be owned by
the emerging agriculturists? Was human society to remain agrarian
and simple, or was it destined to become urban and complex? Should
governance be in the form of small family clans, or should kings rule
from great cities over vast empires?

This tension seems to lurk in the background of the Genesis story
of Cain and Abel. Cain was warned by God to overcome the sin that

was "lurking at the door" (Gen 4:7), but eventually the rivalry erupted into violence as he rose against his brother and slew him in a field. In the millennia to follow there would be rivers of bloodshed flowing through countless battlefields. Cain's killing of Abel was done in secret, but it did not escape the notice of God. When Yahweh confronted Cain, he said,

> "What have you done? Listen, your brother's blood is crying out to me from the ground! And now you are cursed from the ground, which has opened its mouth to receive your brother's blood from your hand." . . . Then Cain went away from the presence of the LORD, and settled in the land of Nod, east of Eden. (Gen 4:10-11, 16)

The shed blood of Abel had a voice, one that invoked a curse upon his brother Cain. Bearing his curse, the first murderer departed from the presence of the Lord and founded the first city (Gen 4:17). Now the pattern for the rise of empire through the bloody conquest of our brothers had been established.

Five generations later the bloody limerick of Lamech gives us a sense of the exponential rise of violence in the antediluvian world.

> Adah and Zillah, hear my voice;
> > you wives of Lamech, listen to what I say:
> I have killed a man for wounding me,
> > a young man for striking me.
> If Cain is avenged sevenfold,
> > truly Lamech seventy-sevenfold. (Gen 4:23-24)

The spiral of ever-increasing violence unleashed by Cain continued until "the earth was corrupt in God's sight, and the earth was filled with violence" (Gen 6:11). And though the flood in the days of Noah may have brough a temporary reprieve, by the time we get to the tower of Babel, the world seems to be no better than it was before the flood. It appears that even divine violence cannot solve the problem of human violence. This is why eventually Abraham was called to leave Ur in search of an alternative—a city not built through the bloodletting violence of Cain and his successors, but a city "whose architect and builder is God" (Heb 11:10). This is the city that Christ constructs. And this is why Jesus would say to a crowd still in the thrall of the one who "was a murderer from the beginning. . . . Your ancestor Abraham rejoiced that he would see my day; he saw it and was glad" (Jn 8:44, 56).

These are the themes of city and sacrifice that the writer of Hebrews plays with in such creative ways. The epistle to the Hebrews, which some scholars think of as an early Christian sermon, draws upon the richness of the Hebrew Bible to set forth Christ as the culmination of the quest of Abraham and the completion of the sacrificial system of Moses. Cain built his city by shedding the blood of his brother. Jesus builds his city by shedding his own blood. The blood of Abel brought a curse upon the offender, but the blood of Jesus speaks a better word than the blood of Abel. The blood of Abel turned Cain into an exiled wanderer, but the blood of Jesus brings us all back home "to the city of the living God, the heavenly Jerusalem" (Heb 12:22).

The goodness of Good Friday is found in the blood that speaks a better word than the blood of Abel. Where the blood of Abel called for vengeance and invoked a curse, the blood of Christ calls for forgiveness and invokes a blessing. When grace is pierced, it bleeds pardon. The blood of Abel drove Cain away from the presence of the Lord to live as an exile east of Eden. The blood of Jesus calls every prodigal son and every wayward daughter back home to the Father's house where the feast of reconciliation is prepared. The singularity of Good Friday means the sin of the world has been forgiven once and for all. The estrangement of exile has been turned into the reconciliation of homecoming.

"But now in Christ Jesus you who once were far off have been brought near by the blood of Christ" (Eph 2:13).

3

GOD REVEALED IN DEATH

When the crucified Jesus is called "the image of the invisible God,"
the meaning is that this is God and God is like this.

JÜRGEN MOLTMANN, *THE CRUCIFIED GOD*

UNTIL THE EMERGENCE OF ATHEISM on a mass scale in late
modernity, everyone believed in God, or more precisely, in the gods.
To account for the phenomenon of existence, the ancients had the
proper instinct to look beyond the crude material world. Thus, every
culture over time developed their own pantheon of transcendent
gods and goddesses who in some way presided over the various phe-
nomena of life and nature. The ancients lived in a world of river gods,
forest gods, lake gods, thunder gods, sun gods, moon gods, and so on.
There were gods of war, gods of fortune, gods of justice, gods of fer-
tility, gods of summer and winter, gods of hearth and home. Every
aspect of life and nature entailed a potential encounter with the
divine. But within these polytheistic religions of the ancient world
there was almost always a supreme god.

In the Egyptian pantheon the supreme deity was Ra, the sun god.
Depicted with the body of a man and the head of a falcon while
holding the *ankh* (key of life), Ra was an unreachable god. As such,
more attention was paid to Osiris, Isis, Horus, and some two

thousand other gods and goddesses. Among the Babylonians, Marduk, the god of thunder, was the supreme deity. He was depicted as a powerful and well-armed warrior able to subdue the monster of chaos. In Zoroastrianism, the Persian religion of antiquity, Ahura Mazda was chief of the gods. Mazda was depicted riding a powerful warhorse with sword in hand, a motif of honorific statuary common even in the modern era. Readers of the Old Testament will be familiar with Baal, the Canaanite lord of storms and fertility. Of course, the most famous among the now retired pagan gods is Zeus, the supreme deity of the Greek pantheon who reigned as king of the gods from Mount Olympus. He is often depicted as standing in a threatening posture holding a thunderbolt. As the king of heaven, Zeus was feared as the god who could and would strike down earthly offenders with his deadly bolts from the heavens. A worshiper would not be inclined to love Zeus but would certainly fear him.

The surviving relics of these erstwhile deities, today displayed in museums, reveal how the gods lived in the minds of their long-ago worshipers, giving us a glimpse into the theology of ancient paganism. The modern visitor to an exhibit of ancient idols observes that the gods of the polytheistic world were depicted as fierce, powerful, and often violent. I have no desire to belittle these worshipers from the distant pagan past, as they had no other way of conceiving the divine. And despite its superstitions, paganism strikes me as a religion every bit as plausible as atheism. Better a world of mercurial gods and goddesses than a world comprised solely of matter unable to account for its own existence.

Yet during the time of the Egyptian, Assyrian, Babylonian, Persian, Greek, and Roman empires and their corresponding religions, there was another people, a unique people who were strange and decidedly different: the Hebrews. The descendants of Abraham worshiped one God and made no image of him, which was unheard of. Every pagan temple housed a pagan idol, but the temple of the Hebrews contained no image of their God. Why? Because in the most revered portion of the Torah was the second of their ten great commandments: "You shall not make for yourself an idol" (Ex 20:4). The God of Israel would remain invisible. The Hebrews worshiped a God they could not see.

At the dedication of Yahweh's temple in Jerusalem, King Solomon proclaimed, "The LORD has said that he would reside in thick darkness" (2 Chron 6:1). On Mount Sinai God told Moses, "You cannot see my face, for no one shall see me and live" (Ex 33:20). And Isaiah declares of Yahweh, "Truly, you are a God who hides himself" (Is 45:15). In the Holy of Holies there was no image, only the ark of the covenant as a throne for the invisible God. This God. unlike the gods of the Gentiles, would not be known by image, but by word. The God of the Torah, the God of the prophets, could not be represented by a graven image.

The Hebrew prohibition against making an image of God was a wise concession to humility. How can mere mortals possibly depict eternal transcendence without error? And to err in depicting the divine is to create an idol—a false and misleading picture of God. No image of God is better than a false image of God.

In the eighth century AD it was Christian zeal for the second of the Ten Commandments that led to the iconoclast movement when icons were destroyed in Byzantine churches by violent fanatics. Fortunately, iconoclasm was an anomaly that could not long endure in Christian theology, as the church made clear at the Seventh Ecumenical Council in 787. The Old Testament prohibition against depicting the divine was a necessary restraint upon human theological presumption that can only create idols. But when God becomes the iconographer and crafts his own perfect icon (image) in the flesh of Christ, this changes everything! Through the incarnation the invisible God of Israel became visible in Jesus of Nazareth. Saint John says, "The Word became flesh and lived among us, and we have seen his glory" (Jn 1:14). Saint Paul says of Christ, "He is the image of the invisible God" (Col 1:15). And the writer of Hebrews says that the Son of God is "the exact imprint of God's very being" (Heb 1:3). Christ is not an idol; he is the perfect icon of the living God.

Ra with his falcon's head, Marduk with his weapons, Mazda upon his warhorse, and Zeus with his hurled thunderbolts are all idols and false images of God. But Christ—the Logos made flesh—is the true icon of the living God. God has now been seen and heard. God has even been touched. As John the Elder says in the opening of his first epistle,

> We declare to you what was from the beginning, what we have *heard*, what we have *seen* with our eyes, what we have *looked at* and *touched* with our hands, concerning the word of life—this life was *revealed*, and we have *seen* it and testify to it and declare to you the eternal life that was with the Father and was revealed to us— what we have *seen* and *heard* we also declare to you so that you also may have fellowship with us, and truly our fellowship is with the Father and with his Son Jesus Christ. (1 Jn 1:1-3, emphasis added)

THIS IS WHAT GOD IS LIKE!

In Jesus Christ the world has at last truly seen God. And what is the climactic, definitive moment of God's self-revelation in Christ? It is the central event in the gospel story—the crucifixion. The crucifixion is the pinnacle of divine self-disclosure. Jesus told the crowds in the temple, "When you lift up the Son of Man, then you will know that I am" (John 8:28 NASB). This is why Paul tells the Corinthian Christians, "For I decided to know nothing among you except Jesus Christ, and him crucified" (1 Cor 2:2). Reflecting on his preaching of the gospel to the Galatian Christians, Paul says, "It was before your eyes that Jesus Christ was publicly exhibited as crucified" (Gal 3:1). When we behold Christ crucified, we can say *this is exactly what God is like!* Being disguised under the disfigurement of an ugly crucifixion and death, Christ upon the cross is paradoxically the clearest revelation of who God is. It's not God in fire upon Mount Sinai or God in glory by the river Chebar, but God in death upon the cross that *fully* reveals who God is. Christ as "the Lamb slain from the foundation of the world" (Rev 13:8 KJV) is not just a historical event. It's who God is.

In his first letter to the Corinthians Paul readily admits that from a human perspective the message of the cross is foolish, even scandalous. Nevertheless, he insists that Christ crucified is the power and wisdom of God and that "God's foolishness is wiser than human wisdom, and God's weakness is stronger than human strength" (1 Cor 1:25). Paul doesn't mean that when God is weak, God is still stronger than human might. That wouldn't be scandalous. It would be just a typical boast about power as conventionally understood. Rather Paul is taking us into the deep mystery of the cross, saying that God's power is precisely located in the weakness we see when we behold God's death upon a cross. The power and wisdom of God are not found in hurled thunderbolts or in some other imagined aspect of omnipotence, but in God nailed to a tree, dying in solidarity with mortal suffering and forgiving the sin of the world. God revealed in weakness and death is what the apostle calls the *mysterion*—"the mystery of Christ" (Eph 3:4). This divine *mysterion* can never be fully fathomed but it is on full display at the cross.

If left to our own assumptions and projections, we will imagine God as unreachably aloof and horribly violent, as our pagan ancestors imagined the gods. But the lifeless body of Christ upon a tree shatters our pagan illusions. At last we have a true image of God. It is a shocking and perhaps unsettling image of God, but it is a true image—the true image.

John the Evangelist, the author of the fourth gospel, was an eyewitness to the crucifixion, and he paints a vivid picture of Christ in death and invites us to gaze upon the pierced one and see God.

> But when they came to Jesus and saw that he was already dead, they did not break his legs. Instead, one of the soldiers pierced his side with a spear, and at once blood and water came out. (He who saw this has testified so that you also may believe. His testimony is true, and he knows that he tells the truth. . . .) These things occurred so that the scripture might be fulfilled, "None of his bones shall be broken." And again another passage

of scripture says, "They will look on the one whom they have pierced." (Jn 19:33-37)

An Eyewitness to the Crucifixion

John's gospel more than any other New Testament book is a literary invitation into the deep mystery of Christ. John is no mere biographer; he is a theologian, and the most mystical of the evangelists. He seems to see things no one else sees in the life of Jesus. John was present at the crucifixion and saw from the pierced side of the dead Christ a stream of blood and water pouring forth. Did no one else see this? Perhaps not, but John is emphatic about the veracity of his witness: "He who saw this has testified so that you may believe. His testimony is true, and he knows that he tells the truth" (Jn. 19:35). John's gospel doesn't so much yield its mysteries to analytical methods as to meditation, which is why so much of it has a poetic feel. It is the original theopoetics of Christ.

Theopoetics beckons us beyond critical textual analysis into contemplative meditation. Unfortunately, modernity is not much inclined toward meditation or metaphor or mystery. Modernity is a tradition that tends to read the Bible only on a literal or historical-critical level, and thus on a shallow and superficial level.

Scripture is not an encyclopedia of God facts, but a portal into the divine mystery. The modernist reading of Scripture is obsessed with facts and information. But more empirical data is not what we need. What we need is a deeper experience with the sacred mystery of Christ. John's strange passage concerning the blood and water flowing from the side of the dead Christ is a prime text to highlight the difference between modern and mystical readings of the Bible. Premodern commentators on the pierced side of Christ see something poignant and precious—a source for mystical meditation. Yet modern commentators want to explain the phenomenon in medical terms, acting as coroners trying to ascertain a forensic cause of death. This is an example of the spiritual poverty that characterizes our pragmatic age. In our determination to make everything practical we have lost the mystical of earlier ages.

Medieval artists found deep inspiration in the scene that John portrays with a few deft sentences in his text. The pierced side of Christ is the subject of the most famous painting of the medieval Greek artist Andreas Pavias (1440–1512). In his *Crucifixion* we behold Christ in death just after his side has been pierced. The cross is absurdly tall, thus giving the impression of Christ spanning earth and heaven. As the blood and water flow, seventeen angels fly around the cross of Christ, fourteen of them depicted in different expressions of grief while the remaining three catch the precious blood and water in chalices. On the top of the cross sits a pelican in a nest, piercing her breast with her beak so she can feed her brood of chicks with her own blood. (The self-sacrificing mother pelican was a common medieval symbol of Christ.) In Pavias's painting, some of the blood of Christ is not caught by the angels in their chalices and flows to the foot of the cross where it falls into the open abyss of hell below, bringing obvious torment to a host of demons. I have no doubt that John the Evangelist would appreciate Andreas Pavias's painting as an appropriate artistic engagement with his own mystical text.

Now compare Pavias's *Crucifixion* with a modern medical drawing of a hemothorax in the pleural cavity used to explain what John saw, and perhaps you can see why a mystical approach to the text will yield far greater riches than a medical analysis. A medical (or historical-critical) reading of the text leads to a single meaning that has little to no bearing upon our lives. A mystical reading of the text leads us into a holy labyrinth where we can explore the mystery of Christ in its multilayered meanings. As we look upon the pierced one as presented to us by John the Evangelist, what do we see? We see God dead upon a tree from whose pierced side there flows a living fountain. John himself connects this with an ancient prophecy from Zechariah:

> And I will pour out a spirit of compassion and supplication on the house of David and the inhabitants of Jerusalem so that, when they look on the one whom they have pierced, they shall mourn for him as one mourns for an only child, and weep bitterly over him as one weeps over a firstborn. . . . On that day a fountain shall be opened for the house of David and the inhabitants of Jerusalem, to cleanse them from sin and impurity. (Zech 12:10; 13:1)

In the spirit of Zechariah's prophecy and John's testimony, the English poet William Cowper wrote this well-known hymn:

> There is a fountain filled with blood
> Drawn from Immanuel's veins
> And sinners plunged beneath that flood
> Lose all their guilty stains.

A WINDOW INTO THE HEART OF GOD

When the early church fathers meditated on the pierced side of Christ, they saw various things. Origen of Alexandria (184–253) saw the rock in the wilderness struck by Moses that brought forth water to save Israel from thirst (Ex 17:1-6). Ephrem the Syrian (306–373) saw the side of the second Adam opened in his deep sleep from which the bride of Christ was brought forth (Gen 2:18-23). Augustine of Hippo (354–430) saw the door set in the side of the ark that provided salvation for all who enter the body of Christ (Gen 6:16; 7:11-16). Ambrose of Milan (340–397) composed a hymn about the pierced side of Christ, where he says,

> At the Lamb's high feast we sing
> Praise to our victorious King,
> Who has washed us in the tide
> Flowing from his pierced side.[1]

The premodern interpreters looked upon the pierced one and saw the sacraments of salvation drawn from the side of Christ. In the water they saw baptism, in the blood they saw the Eucharist. They saw Christ baptizing the world with the cleansing fountain from his side. They saw the world given the saving blood of Christ—the blood we receive in the Eucharist. Each of these spiritual interpretations drawn from an inspired mystical reading of the text is far more edifying than a coroner's report that Jesus of Nazareth died of a hemothorax in the pleural cavity. Only as we engage the mystical text with a mystical reading can we access the true spiritual richness of the Gospels. Don't look with modern eyes and see only a postmortem medical phenomenon. Look with the eyes of faith and try to perceive the spiritual meaning of this miracle.

What do I see when I look upon Christ in death with a pierced side? I see that a soldier's spear has opened a window into the heart of God. As I gaze into the heart of God I discover that there is no wrath, no malice, no threat, no vengeance; only compassion, mercy, and forgiveness. Jesus said, "Out of the abundance of the heart the mouth speaks" (Mt 12:34). Jesus dies, not with a curse upon his lips, but with a plea for pardon. To see Christ upon the cross is to see into the very depths of the heart of God. Where once in our distant pagan past we imagined there lurked monstrous intent threatening harm, we now discover there is only tender compassion. On the cross we encounter a God who would rather die than kill his enemies. When we look through the riven side of Christ into the heart of God, we gaze upon a vast cosmos filled with galaxies of grace.

GOD ON THE GALLOWS

Behind me, I heard the same man asking:
"Where is God now?"
And I heard a voice within me answer him:
"Where is He? Here he is—He is hanging there on this gallows."

Elie Wiesel, *Night*

THE MOST EMOTIVE AND PERSUASIVE ARGUMENT against Judeo-Christian faith is not an argument against the *existence* of God, but an argument against the *goodness* of God. The problem is this: While claiming that God is omniscient and omnipotent, all-good and all-loving, we nevertheless live in a world where the unjust suffering of the innocent is not only possible, but distressingly common. If God is all-knowing, all-powerful, and all-loving, why do babies get brain cancer? The question is wrenching, and as an argument against the goodness of God it can be quite unsettling. The problem of evil is indeed a formidable theological problem—perhaps the greatest theological problem. This is the daunting task of *theodicy*, the vindication of a God of love whose universe permits the existence of evil. But does an adequate theodicy exist?

One of the most potent presentations of the problem of evil as an argument against belief in an all-loving God comes, strangely enough, from the pen of a Christian, Fyodor Dostoevsky. In his masterpiece *The Brothers Karamazov*, Dostoevsky makes his case for Christian faith primarily through the characters of Elder Zosima and his young disciple Alyosha Karamazov. But to his credit, Dostoevsky does not send Zosima and Alyosha into battle against a straw man. Rather he sets forth the problem of evil with all his literary might. Through the character of Ivan Karamazov, Dostoevsky mounts an unsparing attack upon Christian faith.

In the chapter titled "Rebellion," Ivan attempts to subvert the faith of his novice monk brother, Alyosha, by telling three horrific stories that involve the suffering of children. In the first, Ivan tells of soldiers "tossing nursing infants up in the air and catching them on their bayonets before their mothers' eyes."[1] In the second story, Ivan describes sadistic parents who flog their five-year-old daughter, smear her face with excrement, and lock her all night in a freezing outhouse. Ivan then says to Alyosha,

> Can you understand that a small creature, who cannot even comprehend what is being done to her, in a vile place, in the dark and the cold, beats herself on her strained little chest with her tiny fist and weeps with her anguished, gentle, meek tears for "dear God" to protect her—can you understand such nonsense, my friend and my brother, my godly and humble novice, can you understand why this nonsense is needed and created?[2]

In his final story Ivan tells of a general whose house-serf, a boy of eight years, accidently hurt the paw of the general's favorite hunting dog. The boy is discovered and locked up for the night. In the morning,

> The boy is led out of the lockup. A gloomy, cold misty autumn day, a great day for hunting. The general orders them to undress the boy; the child is stripped naked, he shivers, he's crazy with

fear, he doesn't dare make a peep . . . "Drive him!" the general commands. The huntsman shout, "Run, run!" The boy runs . . . "Sic him!" screams the general and looses the whole pack of wolfhounds on him. He hunted him down before his mother's eyes, and the dogs tore the child to pieces![3]

After presenting these three horrific stories involving the suffering of innocent children, Ivan says to his brother, "It's not that I don't accept God, Alyosha, I just most respectfully return him my ticket."[4] Ivan is not directly challenging the existence of God, but asserting that if the Christian God does exist, he cannot possibly be good and therefore Ivan returns his ticket for salvation and any future happiness. The most disturbing thing about this entire gut-wrenching passage is that Dostoevsky did not invent these horrors but drew them from the newspapers. His readers would have known of these terrible crimes. In his attempt to affirm both the goodness of God and the goodness of life, Dostoevsky faces the problem head-on, making his task as difficult as possible. None of the "New Atheists," the cultured despisers of Christianity whose books have become popular in recent decades, have presented a more forceful argument against Christian faith than Fyodor Dostoevsky does through the character of Ivan Karamazov.

But though Ivan's attack is daunting, it's not the last word. Dostoevsky's masterpiece doesn't end with Ivan's attack upon Alyosha's faith. Dostoevsky's affirmation of life and vindication of faith as a response to Ivan's "Rebellion" slowly unfold over the next five hundred pages. Whether or not Dostoevsky successfully overcomes the attack raised by Ivan is for the reader to decide. Dostoevsky is creating art, not propaganda. The final scene in the novel has Alyosha Karamazov returning from the funeral for a nine-year-old boy name Ilyusha Snigeryov. Ilyusha had originally hated the entire Karamazov family including Alyosha, but Alyosha's patient love for

Ilyusha and his impoverished family eventually gave birth to a deep friendship.

Accompanying Alyosha from the funeral are twelve of the deceased boy's young friends. In this remarkable passage, Alyosha functions as a Christ figure speaking to his twelve disciples about the hope of resurrection. Earlier in the novel, Elder Zosima had sent the novice monk Alyosha into the world as an emissary of co-suffering love. Now these boys, once at enmity with Ilyusha, have been drawn together in brotherly harmony through Alyosha's example of love and forgiveness. And this is precisely what Ivan has already rejected. In their tavern conversation Ivan had told his brother,

> Is there in the whole world a being who could and would have the right to forgive? I don't want harmony, for love of mankind I don't want it. I want to remain with unrequited suffering. I'd rather remain with my unrequited suffering and my unquenched indignation, *even if I am wrong.*[5]

Elder Zosima taught Alyosha the very opposite of Ivan's embittered philosophy. Instead of railing against sin and injustice, Zosima taught Alyosha to take personal responsibility for the unjust suffering of the world and to seek to heal it through unconditional love.

In his homilies Zosima says,

> Do not be afraid of men's sin. Love man also in his sin, for this likeness of God's love is the height of love on earth. . . . There is only one salvation for you: take yourself up, and make yourself responsible for all the sins of men. For indeed it is so, my friend, and the moment you make yourself sincerely responsible for everything and everyone, you will see at once that it really is so, that it is you who are guilty on behalf of all and for all. Whereas by shifting your own laziness and powerlessness onto others, you will end by sharing in Satan's pride and murmuring against God. . . . If the wickedness of

people arouses indignation and insurmountable grief in you, to the point that you desire to revenge yourself upon the wicked, fear that feeling most of all. . . . Believe that if they are not saved now, they will be saved later. . . . Your work is for the whole, your deed is for the future.[6]

It is to these twelve children, now returning from the funeral of their friend, that Alyosha has taught the lessons of co-suffering love he learned from Elder Zosima. The novel ends like this:

"Karamazov!" cried Kolya, "can it really be true as religion says, that we shall all rise from the dead and come to life, and see one another again, and everyone, and Ilyushechka?"

"Certainly we shall rise, certainly we shall see and gladly, joyfully tell one another all that has been," Alyosha replied, half laughing, half in ecstasy.

"Ah, how good that will be!" burst Kolya.

"Well, and now, let's end our speeches and go to his memorial dinner. Don't be disturbed that we'll be eating pancakes. It's an ancient, eternal thing, and there's good in that, too," laughed Alyosha. "Well, let's go! And we go like this now, hand in hand."

"And eternally so, all our lives hand in hand! Hurrah for Karamazov!" Kolya cried once more ecstatically and once more all the boys joined in his exclamation.[7]

As I said, the reader will have to decide whether Dostoevsky successfully achieves his goal of underscoring God's goodness, even while permitting a world of evil, but I will say there is a reason why *The Brothers Karamazov* is not only my favorite novel, but perhaps my favorite theological work as well—and I'm not alone in this assessment. No work of fiction has rivaled its influence on contemporary theology. Yet eighty years later another book was published that we must take very seriously when considering the thorny question of theodicy. That book is *Night* by Elie Wiesel.

NIGHT

Elie Wiesel (1928–2016) was a Romanian-born Jew and Nobel laureate who survived the death camps of Auschwitz and Buchenwald as a teenager. The rest of his family, however, perished in the Holocaust. His father died at Buchenwald in the bunk above him after a brutal beating from a Nazi guard. Among the millions of human victims murdered by Hitler in the Holocaust, there was yet another victim—Elie Wiesel's faith in God. In *Night* he writes, "Never shall I forget those moments which murdered my God and my soul and turned my dreams to dust. Never shall I forget these things, even if I am condemned to live as long as God Himself. Never."[8] For me, the most agonizing passage in this darkest of books is when Wiesel vividly describes the hanging of two men and a boy. Describing the young boy Wiesel writes, "He had the face of a sad angel."[9] Adding to the barbarity of it all, the SS guards forced the prisoners to watch the hangings and then to file past the victims upon the gallows. Wiesel describes it like this:

> Then the march began. The two adults were no longer alive. Their tongues hung swollen, blue-tinged. But the third rope was still moving; being so light, the child was still alive. . . .
>
> For more than half an hour he stayed there, struggling between life and death, dying in slow agony under our eyes. And we had to look him full in the face. He was still alive when I passed in front of him. His tongue was still red, his eyes were not yet glazed.
>
> Behind me, I heard the same man asking:
>
> "Where is God now?"
>
> And I heard a voice within me answer him:
>
> "Where is He? Here He is—He is hanging there on this gallows."[10]

With the death of this boy died Elie Wiesel's faith in God. And I cannot think of a passage in all of literature that more starkly presents the problem of theodicy. Where is God when Nazis hang a boy with the face of a sad angel? What kind of possible theodicy can be offered in response to such crimes? Does the Bible even attempt to rise to the challenge? The Psalms make it clear that the Bible is aware of the problem of the suffering of the innocent, but does it offer an adequate answer?

The Book of Job, for all its wisdom, is not a theodicy. It's a poignant wisdom poem portraying the absurd suffering of a righteous man. Job's suffering is compounded by the failed theodicy of his friends who attempt to justify God by blaming the sufferer. As the *satan* (the Hebrew word for accuser) migrates into the minds and words of Job's friends, they become cruel, satan-possessed tormentors. The Book of Job may teach us how to argue with God and perhaps even how to trust God, but it does not offer an adequate theodicy. Rather, it eloquently sets forth the problem of unjust suffering and concludes with the hope of an eschatological restoration, but nothing in the great poem attempts to justify God—not even in the over-awing whirlwind speeches that silence Job. So as a plausible response to the problem of evil is there any theodicy at all found in Scripture? There is, but only one.

A THEOLOGY AFTER AUSCHWITZ

Where is God in unspeakable human suffering? He is there, hanging on the gallows. If authentic being requires a radical freedom where all things are permitted, including unmitigated evil, God does not exempt himself from the experience, but fully shares it with us in Christ. The only theodicy I know is that God, too, has hung, suffered, and died upon the gallows. In solidarity with the sad angel of Buchenwald, God, too, has been gazed upon in death throes.

Luke tells of those who witnessed the death of Jesus at Golgotha: "And when all the crowds who had gathered there for this spectacle saw what had taken place, they returned home, beating their breasts. But all his acquaintances, including the women who had followed him from Galilee, stood at a distance watching these things" (Lk 23:48-49). Ultimately, that which sustains faith in a world of suffering is the eschatological hope for the restoration of all things. This is the blessed hope of *apokatastasis*, the beautiful Greek word translated "universal restoration" in Acts 3:21.

With this hope we look for the dawn of a new creation where death is undone and suffering and sorrow are no more.

> So when I'm walking this prison camp world
> I long for a glimpse of the new life unfurled
> The chrysalis is cracking and moistened wings uncurl
> Like in the vision John saw[11]

But as we await the arrival of the new Jerusalem in a prison camp world that languishes between fallen creation and new creation, we find comfort in the truth that God in Christ has entered into all human suffering with full solidarity. Where is God? He is not aloof and impassible; he is hanging on the gallows with all who suffer. The agony of unjust suffering, the kind described by Elie Wiesel, the kind endured by millions of sufferers, does not lie outside the actual human experience of God. Is this an adequate theodicy? Maybe, maybe not, but it's the only one I know of that approaches any measure of satisfaction.

When we see Christ in agony upon the cross, we see a suffering God who refuses to allow his beloved creatures to suffer alone. I believe this helps enormously. As Dietrich Bonhoeffer famously wrote, prior to himself being hanged upon Nazi gallows, "Only the suffering God can help."[12] Aristotle's God as the "Unmoved Mover" who sits impassibly on high is of no help to those who suffer. This is the impotency of a God who is merely omnipotent. Jürgen Moltmann describes it like this:

A God who is only omnipotent is in himself an incomplete being, for he cannot experience helplessness and powerlessness. Omnipotence can indeed be longed for and worshipped by helpless men, but omnipotence is never loved; it is only feared. What sort of being, then, would be a God who was only "almighty"? He would be a being without experience, a being without destiny and a being who is loved by no one. A man who experiences helplessness, a man who suffers because he loves, a man who can die, is therefore a richer being than an omnipotent God who cannot suffer, cannot love and cannot die.[13]

Such is not the Christian God—for our God loves and suffers and is only fully known as God in the crucified Son of Man. In the crucified one we find the suffering God who helps us endure our own suffering and to find meaning in what threatens to be meaningless suffering. The cross is more than solidarity with human suffering, but it's not less than that. And it's far more than an empty gesture of solidarity.

Christian faith confesses that somehow the boy with the face of a sad angel hung upon Nazi gallows is taken up into the suffering of Christ and healed. The boy is not abandoned, he is not left alone, he is not left unhealed. Peter's sacred testimony is that by the wounds of Christ we are healed (1 Pet 2:24), and our most robust Christian hope is that this is ultimately true for all human sufferers. Christ has entered Auschwitz and Auschwitz has entered Christ. If Christ assumes humanity to heal humanity, this includes Auschwitz. The Holocaust is not permitted to be the final word on theology or theodicy. Again, Jürgen Moltmann:

A "theology after Auschwitz" may seem an impossibility or blasphemy to those who allowed themselves to be satisfied with theism or their childhood beliefs and then lost them. And there would be no "theology after Auschwitz" in retrospective sorrow and the recognition of guilt, had there been no "theology in Auschwitz." Anyone who later comes up against insoluble problems and despair must remember that the *Shema* of Israel and the Lord's Prayer were prayed in Auschwitz.[14]

Elie Wiesel's *Night* has been translated into thirty languages and sold over ten million copies. Other than *The Diary of Anne Frank*, it is probably the most read work in the history of Holocaust literature.

It ends with Wiesel seeing his image in a mirror after the liberation of Buchenwald—the first time he had seen his reflection since entering the concentration camps: "From the depths of the mirror, a corpse gazed back at me. The look in his eyes, as they stared into mine, has never left me."[15]

Night is a book about death wrought by unspeakable evil—including the death of God. But *Night* is not the end of Elie Wiesel's story. In the 1980s, then in his fifties, Elie Wiesel began to write differently. In books like *Souls on Fire* and *Messengers for God*, Wiesel explored the human experience of engaging with the living God. Wiesel's murdered faith had begun to resurrect. Eugene Peterson tells of hearing Elie Wiesel speak in Baltimore around this time: "He spent the next hour leading us, a secular audience of seven or eight hundred people, in what was essentially a Bible study. Everything he said could have been transcribed from a Wednesday night prayer meeting in a Baptist church."[16] The God who died in Elie Wiesel's death camp experience had risen again.

After hearing Wiesel speak with conviction about the God of Abraham, Isaac, and Jacob, Peterson writes, "A person can go through the worst, have every shred of faith pulled away from the soul, leaving it bare and shivering in a world where all the evidence gives proof that God is dead, and still become a person of faith."[17] God has been hung upon the gallows. God has drunk the bitter dregs of human depravity. God has died a degrading death at the hands of cruel oppressors. But God is not dead. Indeed, the *Shema* and the Lord's Prayer really were prayed in Auschwitz. And from the dungeons of Nero and Diocletian to the death camps of Hitler and Stalin, suffering believers have drawn comfort from the God who has suffered with them.

THE ROAD
OF DISCIPLESHIP

*I paint the comfortable Christ, with a halo over his head. How can I show
what I haven't lived? Someday I might have the courage to venture.
Not yet.*

A HIDDEN LIFE

JESUS RECRUITED HIS DISCIPLES with a simple but de-
manding imperative: "Follow me" (Mk 2:14). This terse call to
discipleship occurs no less than twenty times in the Gospels. What
does it mean to be a disciple of Jesus? It means to heed the call to
follow him. And it implies that in following Jesus we will travel a
road that we would not have chosen for ourselves. The first among
the disciples to confess Jesus as the Messiah was Simon Peter, a fisher-
man who left his nets to follow Jesus. In response, Jesus, for the first
time, reveals the true *telos*, the ultimate aim of his messianic mission:
that when they reach Jerusalem he will be rejected by the elders,
condemned by the chief priests, handed over to the Romans for
execution, and raised on the third day.

That the messianic mission of their rabbi would culminate in his
crucifixion was *not* something Jesus' first followers had imagined or

bargained for. Thus, the impetuous Peter takes it upon himself to rebuke Jesus by saying, "God forbid it, Lord! This must never happen to you" (Mt 16:22). Jesus' retort is swift and severe: "Get behind me, Satan" (Mt 16:23). The temptation to save the world while evading the cross first came to Jesus in the wilderness directly from Satan, and now it comes through the lips of his most prominent disciple. This temptation will return one final time in Gethsemane. Despite its seductiveness, Jesus always identified the impulse to achieve glory apart from the cross as satanic in origin. Having rebuked Peter's suggestion of a cross-less Christ, Jesus now sets forth the terms of discipleship for all his would-be followers. Calling the crowd and his disciples near, he said to them, "If any wish to come after me, let them deny themselves and take up their cross and follow me" (Mk 8:34).

It is nearly impossible for us to comprehend just how shocking Jesus' words were to his Jewish audience in the first century. We are accustomed to making a casual religious association between the words *cross* and *disciple*. But to his original hearers, Christ's association of crucifixion with discipleship would have bordered on the outrageous. A disciple might be called to take up his prayer shawl, but his *cross*?! There was nothing religious or spiritual about a cross—it was ugly and profane. It was known only as a horrible instrument of execution employed by the Roman Empire to inflict the most degrading death upon slaves and rebels. The Bible itself seems to recoil at the idea of being hanged on a tree. As the Torah says, "Anyone hung on a tree is under God's curse" (Deut 21:23). When Jesus said to prospective disciples, "Take up your cross and follow me," it would not have been heard as a call to a pious spirituality. It could only be understood as a call to martyrdom. And what could be more shocking than that?

In 1505 the Dutch painter Hieronymus Bosch completed *Christ Carrying the Cross*. In the painting Jesus wears a crown of thorns as he struggles under the weight of the cross. The most striking aspect of the painting is how Jesus looks directly at the viewer as a single tear rolls down his cheek. The viewer can almost hear Jesus say, "Follow me."

As Jesus announced the imminent arrival of the kingdom of God, his disciples clearly assumed there would come a time to take up the sword in the manner of Joshua and David and Judah Maccabee. When Jesus was arrested in the Garden of Gethsemane, his disciples shouted, "Lord, should we strike with the sword?" (Lk 22:49)—and then proceeded to do so. But no. Jesus' renunciation of the sword was clear: "No more of this" (Lk 22:51). Rather than take up the sword, he would instead embrace the cross. Jesus was willing to die for that which he was unwilling to kill.

This is the context in which Jesus says, "Follow me." He calls his disciples to lay down the sword and take up the cross—to renounce violence and embrace martyrdom. The kingdom of God is a direct challenge to pagan empire, and thus the kingdom of God cannot come by the lethal ways of Pharaoh and Caesar and all their successors. God's kingdom will advance not by spilling the blood of enemies, but the blood of martyrs. The spectacle that embodies the kingdom of heaven will not be the military parades typical of the imperial Roman triumphs, but the condemned Christ carrying his cross to Golgotha. The temptation to make Christianity about a warrior's triumph instead of a martyr's death is what Martin Luther described as the opposing theologies of glory and cross. Walter Brueggemann explains it like this:

> As long ago as the sixteenth century, Martin Luther boldly voiced a vigorous either/or for Christian faith in terms of a "Theology of Glory" and a "Theology of the Cross." By the former Luther referred to an articulation of Gospel faith that smacked of triumphalism that was allied with worldly power that specialized in winning, control, being first, and being best. For Luther, that theology was all tied up with the European

imperial of his time. By the contrast of a "Theology of the Cross," Luther referred to the risky way of Jesus that is marked by humility, obedience, and vulnerability standing in sharp contrast to and in opposition to the hunger for "Glory." The "way of the cross," for Luther, is demanding and costly because it contradicts the dominant way of the world.[1]

THE WAY OF MARTYRDOM

Contradicting the dominant way of the world is what following Jesus on the demanding road of discipleship is about. We walk that road shouldering our cross, not our rifle. This is the enduring model of discipleship. The way of Christian discipleship is to deny the primal but fallen instinct to prioritize our own security and self-interest, and to voluntarily imitate what Jesus did with the cross. In Christian discipleship the cross is not only something Jesus did for us, but also the pattern we are to follow. As Christians we don't just stand on the sidelines and watch Jesus carry his cross. No, we fall in behind and carry our own cross. The cross is the call to self-denial for the sake of imitating Christ. For most of us, the cross of self-denial for the sake of Christ will not lead to actual martyrdom at the hands of the enemies of truth, but for some it will. And for every Christian, the possibility of martyrdom is always on the table. Indeed, in the Greek New Testament the word for witness (*martys*) is also the word for martyr. The call to be a witness for Christ is by implication a call to the possibility of being his martyr.

For the early church, martyrdom was an existential reality and an ever-present possibility. This continues to be the case for millions of Christians living in authoritarian regimes and religious cultures hostile to their faith. But for many American Christians, martyrdom is viewed not only as unthinkable, but perhaps even as disgraceful. Americans are so smitten with the lore of cowboy justice, where all wrongs are set right by a hero with a trusty six-shooter, that the notion of dying instead of killing is perceived as weak and ignoble.

In American evangelical churches you are far more likely to find celebrations of military might than you are to hear stories of the early Christian martyrs. In these churches John Wayne is more valorized than Justin Martyr. The loss of memory regarding the martyrs is a particular form of Protestant poverty. But this is what happens when a theology of glory eclipses a theology of the cross. We need to be startled out of our malaise by the jarring words of Dietrich Bonhoeffer: "When Christ calls a man, he bids him come and die."[2]

In his classic work *The Cost of Discipleship*, published in Berlin in 1937, Bonhoeffer writes,

> To endure the cross is not a tragedy; it is the suffering which is the fruit of an exclusive allegiance to Jesus Christ. When it comes, it is not an accident, but a necessity. It is not the sort of suffering which is inseparable from this mortal life, but the suffering which is an essential part of the specifically Christian life. It is not suffering *per se* but suffering-and-rejection for the sake of Christ. . . . But this notion has ceased to be intelligible to a Christianity which can no longer see any difference between ordinary human life and a life committed to Christ.[3]

Bonhoeffer was not writing abstract theology in a political vacuum; he was writing in the shadow of the Nazi swastika and Adolf Hitler's rise to power. When he writes that the suffering of the cross is the result of "an exclusive allegiance to Jesus Christ," he is addressing millions of people in the German Christian Movement who naïvely thought they could combine an allegiance to Christ and his kingdom with an allegiance to Hitler and German nationalism.

German evangelicals had deluded themselves into thinking that if Nazism was anti-communist, it must be Christian. They had conflated the cause of German nationalism with Christian evangelism. Because they had heard it preached from their pulpits, they believed that the supremacy of the German nation was God's will. With *Gott mit uns*—God with us—on their belt buckles, baptized Nazis goose-stepped in military parades. Millions of German Christians felt no contradiction attending a Nazi rally on Saturday night before attending church on Sunday morning.

But Bonhoeffer knew better. The kind of grace dispensed in a Nazi-supporting church is what Bonhoeffer derided as "cheap grace." His book on discipleship opens with these words: "Cheap grace is the deadly enemy of our Church. We are fighting today for costly grace."[4] For Bonhoeffer, viewing the cross as something solely belonging to Christ, by which we are given the grace of forgiveness regardless of any intention to imitate Christ in his suffering, is cheap grace. "Cheap grace is the grace we bestow on ourselves. . . . Cheap grace is grace without discipleship, grace without the cross."[5] By grace without the cross, Bonhoeffer means grace without taking up a cross in imitation of Christ, without sharing in the suffering of Christ. And the highest form of Christlike suffering is martyrdom.

Bonhoeffer writes,

> Jesus says that every Christian has his own cross waiting for him, a cross destined and appointed by God. Each must endure his allotted share of suffering and rejection. But each has a different share: some God deems worthy of the highest form of suffering, and gives them the grace of martyrdom.[6]

These are not mere aspirational sentiments about the cost of discipleship. Bonhoeffer gave himself over to them in the last full measure of devotion. Eight years after he wrote about "the grace of martyrdom," he found that grace at the end of a Nazi noose. He was thirty-nine.

Dietrich Bonhoeffer came from one of Berlin's most prestigious families—his father was a famous psychiatrist. Bonhoeffer's work as a brilliant theologian, along with his arrest, imprisonment, and martyrdom were all widely known. But there were others whose courageous faith and martyr's death were largely hidden from public knowledge. Others like Franz Jägerstätter.

FRANZ JÄGERSTÄTTER

Franz Jägerstätter (1907–1943) was an Austrian farmer in the small mountain village of St. Radegund on the German-Austrian border. In his youth he had a reputation for being something of a trouble-maker and womanizer. He was prone to gang fights and scrapes with police. But around age twenty-nine, Jägerstätter experienced a pro-found spiritual awakening—a sudden conversion that surprised the people of St. Radegund who knew him as a motorcycle-riding hoo-ligan. Jägerstätter's religious conversion was characterized by a deep love for the Scriptures as he read the Bible obsessively, often dis-cussing texts with the village priest. His immersion in the Scriptures led him to reject the growing popularity of Nazism among his fellow Austrians. Jägerstätter saw Hitler as an antichrist leading deceived souls to hell, and as a result was gradually ostracized by his fellow villagers for not being sufficiently patriotic.

After the German annexation of Austria in 1938, Austrian con-scripts into the German army were required to swear an oath of al-legiance to Hitler. Jägerstätter refused. He was the only man in his village to do so and was promptly arrested on March 1, 1943. During his five months of imprisonment, Jägerstätter was repeatedly offered release upon condition of signing the oath of allegiance. He stead-fastly refused. On August 9, 1943, Jägerstätter was executed by guil-lotine in Brandenburg Prison. His last words were, "I am completely bound in inner union with the Lord."[7] He was thirty-six years old.

In the years following WWII, his martyrdom was almost entirely unknown outside his tiny Austrian village. And in St. Radegund, even after the war, Jägerstätter's refusal to fight for the Nazis was not generally celebrated. In 1964, Gordon Zahn published a biography of Jägerstätter, titled *In Solitary Witness*. At last the Christian world began to learn the story of this remarkable martyr. In 1997 the German government symbolically nullified his death sentence, and in 2007 he was beatified by Pope Benedict XVI, placing him on the path to Catholic sainthood. His wife (then age ninety-four) and his four daughters were present for the beatification ceremony.

In 2019, the film *A Hidden Life* was released. Written and directed by acclaimed filmmaker Terrence Malick, it tells the story of Franz Jägerstätter's life and martyrdom. In December of 2019 I saw the film at an art theater in Kansas City and have since watched this three-hour movie at least twenty times. It's influence on me has been profound. *A Hidden Life* is an exquisitely beautiful and deeply powerful portrayal of Christian faith set against the backdrop of horrific evil. Father John Dear, a Jesuit priest, peace activist, and close friend of the Jägerstätter family, told me the film was a faithful depiction of Jägerstätter's life and death.

Although the film generally received positive reviews, winning two prizes at the Cannes Film Festival, not all feedback was positive. I read one review where the critic said he couldn't understand why Franz Jägerstätter did what he did. It caused me to wonder if the critic had slept through the entire film. Without turning into cloying propaganda, Malick goes to great artistic lengths to portray Jägerstätter's conscientious objection as an expression of Christian faith. Images of churches and crucifixes are constantly in the background of the film—by my count in over one hundred scenes! Yet in the plot of the film, the church itself is depicted in contradictory ways. Sometimes the church seems to be a source for Jägerstätter's faith, but more often the clergy try to weaken his resolve. Yet other times bishops and priests speak to him about duty to his family and nation, citing Romans 13 as biblical warrant for baptized Christians joining the German army.

In one of my favorite scenes in the film, Jägerstätter visits a church while his friend Ohlendorf, an artist, paints frescos on the walls. The two friends converse about the dark time they are living through. As Ohlendorf stands on a scaffold, painting scenes from the life of Christ, he says to Jägerstätter,

I paint all this suffering, but I don't suffer myself. I make a living of it. What we do is just create admirers, we don't create followers. Christ's life is a demand. We don't want to be reminded of it. . . . I paint the comfortable Christ, with a halo over his head. How can I show what I haven't lived? Someday I might have the courage to venture. Not yet.[8]

The first time I saw the movie, I immediately recognized where Terrence Malick got his inspiration for these lines. They come from the Danish philosopher and Christian thinker Søren Kierkegaard. Terrence Malick is a Rhodes scholar with a degree in philosophy from Harvard University. Before turning to filmmaking, he was preparing for a career in philosophy with an emphasis on Hegel, Kierkegaard, and Wittgenstein. Malick knows his Kierkegaard, and the great Dane's philosophy shows up in many of Malick's films.

Here's an example of what Kierkegaard wrote concerning admirers and followers of Christ.

What then is the difference between an admirer and a follower? A follower *is* or strives *to be* what he admires. An admirer, however, keeps himself personally detached. He fails to see that what is admired involves a claim upon him, and thus he fails to be or strive to be what he admires. . . . Admirers are only all too willing to serve Christ as long as proper caution is exercised, lest one personally come in contact with danger. As such, they refuse to accept that Christ's life is a demand. . . . When there is no danger, when there is a dead calm, when everything is favorable to our Christianity, it is all too easy to confuse an admirer with a follower. And this can happen very quietly. The admirer can be in the delusion that the position he takes is the true one, when all he is doing is playing it safe. Give heed, therefore, to the call of discipleship![9]

The difference between admirers and followers of Christ is essentially the plotline so deftly portrayed in *A Hidden Life*. The devout church-attending villagers of St. Radegund were *admirers* of Christ. Franz Jägerstätter was a *follower* of Christ. The admirers avoided contact with danger, seeming entirely reasonable in doing so. The lone follower was obedient to Christ despite the danger—and he seems either a fool or a saint, depending on our point of view.

I don't think it is too much of a stretch to say that Terrence Malick has placed himself in the film as the character of Ohlendorf—the Kierkegaard-quoting painter who makes a living creating beautiful images. "How can I show what I haven't lived? Someday I might have the courage to venture. Not yet." In the light of Jägerstätter's martyrdom, does Malick wonder if he himself is a follower of Christ or merely an admirer? It's the question the film should evoke in each of us. All I can say is I have sincere respect for Malick's humble self-reflection. And I deeply appreciate his prodigious artistic prowess summoned to tell the world of an Austrian farmer's martyrdom. The film ends with a quote from George Eliot reminding us that much of the good in this world is due to those who faithfully lived and died a hidden life: "For the growing good of the world is partly dependent on unhistoric acts; and that things are not so ill with you and me as they might have been, is half owing to the number who lived faithfully, a hidden life, and rest in unvisited tombs."[10]

6

A LOVE SUPREME

Lovers are the ones who know the most about God;
the theologians must listen to them.

HANS URS VON BALTHASAR, *LOVE ALONE IS CREDIBLE*

ON DECEMBER 9, 1964, the great jazz saxophonist John Coltrane recorded *A Love Supreme* in a single session. It is Coltrane's masterpiece and universally recognized as one of the greatest jazz recordings of all time. The four tracks on this thirty-four-minute album are all titled "A Love Supreme," with each given a different subtitle: "Acknowledgement," "Resolution," "Pursuance," and "Psalm." *A Love Supreme* is an instrumental album—the only vocals are on the first track where Coltrane chants nineteen times, "A love supreme."

In the liner notes Coltrane writes,

DEAR LISTENER: ALL PRAISE BE TO GOD TO WHOM ALL PRAISE IS DUE. Let us pursue Him in the righteous path. Yes it is true; "seek and ye shall find." Only through Him can we know the most wondrous bequeathal. During the year 1957, I experienced, by the grace of God, a spiritual awakening which was to lead me to a richer, fuller, more productive life. . . . ALL PRAISE TO GOD. HE IS GRACIOUS AND MERCIFUL. HIS

WAY IS IN LOVE, THROUGH WHICH WE ALL ARE. IT IS
TRULY—A LOVE SUPREME—.[1]

Though jazz is not my primary musical muse, *A Love Supreme* is an
album I return to time and again. My soul senses the transcendent
sacred in Coltrane's music. It's the kind of music that traces the inef-
fable. The poetic and prophetic are related, as are music and magic.
Where prose fails, poetry must take up the task. And where poetry
fails, perhaps only music will do. Like Johann Sebastian Bach, John
Coltrane is one of those angelic artists whose music tells us some-
thing about God. And I'm not alone in this opinion. Public intel-
lectual and Christian theologian Cornel West cites John Coltrane as
one of his primary influences.

In his memoir, West writes,

> I'm fortified by long listening sessions with the sanctified music of
> John Coltrane. Trane: another celestial genius whose sacred voice
> gives me hope. And by hope I mean blues-inflicted hope that is
> morally sound; hope earned in the harsh realities of daily struggle;
> hope that remains on intimate terms with death; hope that is life-
> renewing and opposed to the cheap optimism of market-driven
> America where Disneyland is sold as heaven on earth. . . . [Col-
> trane] did not define his spirituality, as I did, in terms of Jesus
> Christ or Christian faith. But that didn't matter because his artistic
> muse—what he called "A Love Supreme"—had us walking down
> parallel paths. He led me to the same places as the preaching of my
> childhood minister, the Reverend Willie P. Cooke.[2]

The one thing all mystics seem to have in common is a spiritual rev-
elation that God is love. Whether it's Jewish mystics, Christian
mystics, Sufi mystics, or jazz mystics, they all carry a profound sense
of what John Coltrane called "A Love Supreme." And for Christians,
a love supreme is intuitively connected to the cross as the supreme
act of divine love. How we interpret the connection between a love

supreme and Christ's death upon the cross is not always clear and has long been a subject of theological debate. But Christian Scripture, theology, and mysticism have all passionately affirmed that there is a real connection between the cross of Christ and the love of God. Christians have always confessed that Golgotha is not just the scene of the greatest crime, it is also the site of a love supreme.

BIG LOVE IN THE CHURCH OF THE HOLY SEPULCHRE

For seventeen centuries Christians have worshiped at the Church of the Holy Sepulchre in Jerusalem. In Christian tradition it is the site of both the crucifixion and resurrection of Jesus Christ. Having spent countless hours there, I am intimately acquainted with the space. To reach the Golgotha chapel, the worshiper climbs the steep, winding stairs just inside the church's entrance. Stone steps worn with deep concaves bear testimony to the millions of pilgrims who have come to this holy place. Situated next to the Golgotha rock is a beautiful mosaic that depicts Christ being nailed to the cross. On one of our many visits there, my wife photographed a detail of the mosaic in which Jesus' nail-pierced right hand produces a trickle of blood. The artist created the mosaic with a combination of black, brown, green, yellow, beige, white, pink, and red colored stones. Despite the macabre subject matter, both the mosaic and the photograph are beautiful. Years ago I saved Peri's photograph to my computer with the name "Big Love." It's these pierced hands that John Coltrane called "A Love Supreme."

The golden thread of the New Testament is the recurring theme of divine love—and this love reaches its supreme expression in the Son of God laying down his life. Here are some of the more well-known texts in the Epistles that connect Jesus' death on the cross with divine love:

- But God proves his love for us in that while we still were sinners Christ *died* for us. (Rom 5:8, emphasis added)

- I live by the faith of the Son of God, who loved me and *gave himself* for me. (Gal 2:20)

- Christ loved us and *gave himself* up for us. (Eph 5:2)

- We know love by this, that he *laid down his life* for us. (1 Jn 3:16)

- To him who loved us and freed us from our sins *by his blood*. (Rev 1:5)

Jesus himself spoke of his impending death as a supreme act of love, when on the eve of his suffering he said to his disciples, "There is no greater love than to lay down one's life for one's friends" (Jn 15:13 NLT). And when Jesus made a clear allusion to his death by crucifixion in telling Nicodemus, "Just as Moses lifted up the serpent in the wilderness, so must the Son of Man be lifted up" (Jn 3:14), the commentary that follows is the most famous verse in the Bible: "For God so loved the world that he gave his only Son" (Jn 3:16). The Sunday school hymn says, "Jesus loves me this I know for the Bible tells me so." And the Bible tells of Jesus' love for us by telling how he died for us. How do we know God loves us? We know because Jesus died for us.

Liberal theology over the last couple of centuries has often tried to separate the teaching ministry of Jesus from his suffering and death. In this thinking, the teachings of Jesus were the essence of his life and ministry, and the crucifixion was nothing but a tragic catastrophe. The wisdom teacher of Nazareth was the unfortunate victim of the machinations of bad religion and cruel empire. In these forms of liberal theology, it's as if Jesus began proclaiming a gospel of love only to have it all go absurdly wrong at the end, the assumption being that the cross was an unanticipated end for a teacher of love.

But this thought must be rejected out of hand. As Hans Urs von Balthasar has said, "We cannot take seriously any attempt to separate Jesus' teaching before the Passion."[3] Once Jesus has preached the Sermon on the Mount, to *live* his own sermon will establish a trajectory that will take him from the Mount of Beatitudes to Mount

Calvary. Love of God, love of neighbor, and love of enemy find their fullest expression in the self-emptying sacrifice of death. In a world built upon the greed of empire, the violence of war, and the hatred of enemy, a life lived according to the supremacy of love can only end at the cross.

The Gospels make it clear that Jesus knew his fate was to be crucified in Jerusalem. By at least the midpoint of his ministry (the transfiguration), Jesus plainly tells his disciples that he will be killed. But we have reason to suspect Jesus knew of the cross as early as his baptism. The wilderness temptations can be interpreted as satanically suggested alternatives to the cross—to save the world through bread, spectacle, and conquest. Despite knowing his fate, Jesus moves resolutely toward the cross because he is compelled by love. Jesus was not crucified as a naive, hapless victim, but as a martyr of love. As he said, "The good shepherd lays down his life for the sheep" (Jn 10:11). From the moment Jesus began his public ministry he was headed for the cross. "Having loved his own who were in the world, he loved them to the end" (Jn 13:1).

The death of Christ upon the cross was an act of love supreme, and it was not merely a gesture of solidarity with all who suffer in a world forged in hate. Jesus was *saving* the world—and he was saving it in the only way the world could be saved. For sin and death to be defeated, Jesus had to drink the bitter cup. There was no other way. And all of this plays out in an arena of love. Love alone provides the motive for the Paschal drama. Without love as the metanarrative, the crucifixion of Jesus of Nazareth becomes a nihilistic absurdity. But the gospel is not an absurdist tragedy.

Jesus goes to the cross with his eyes wide open and his heart full of love. He says, "For this reason the Father loves me, because I lay down my life in order to take it up again" (Jn 10:17). But it must be emphasized that Jesus' death was not simply an act of loving solidarity with all who suffer and die, for in taking up his life again, Jesus takes the whole world up with him. The apostle Paul speaks of the saving love of Christ like this: "For the love of Christ urges us on, because we are convinced that one has died for all; therefore all have died. And he died for all, so that those who live might live no longer for themselves but for the one who for their sake died and was raised" (2 Cor 5:14-15).

Compelled by love Jesus died for all that all might be made alive in his resurrection. This is the mystery of redemption. This is the hope of *apokatastasis*—the "universal restoration" spoken of by the apostle Peter (Acts 3:21). Jesus himself spoke of the saving power of his love-compelled death when he said, "And I, when I am lifted up from the earth, will draw all people to myself" (Jn 12:32). Once a symbol of imperial terror, the cross has become the eternal symbol of divine love. When we look upon a cross today, we don't see an instrument of torture and death; we see the supreme demonstration of God's love. We see the lengths to which God will go to save the world.

When we speak of the suffering love on display at the cross, we must be careful not to isolate this suffering in the Son of God alone. There are some theologies of the cross that make the mistake of imagining the Father as entirely aloof and impassible to the suffering of the Son. Or worse, there are atonement theologies that posit the Father as the *source* of the Son's suffering. This is paganized soteriology at its worst! The Father is not the one who inflicts pain and suffering upon the Son. To imagine the Father as the one inflicting pain upon the Son is to import an unspeakable violence into the Trinity. The Father, Son, and Holy Spirit are bound together in eternal love. In the crucifixion of the Son, the Trinity shares the suffering. The Trinity does not consist of separate parts with separate experiences. The Trinity has no "parts." The Trinity is the divine community in a perichoretic dance of love.

The Swiss physician and mystic Adrienne von Speyr says it like this: "The suffering on the Cross is the expression of the love within God. The expression chosen by God to show us his love; in order to be able to reveal itself, love suffers."[4]

GRIEF IS WOUNDED LOVE

To love someone is to share in their suffering. Grief is wounded love. Where there is no love there can be no empathetic grief. Certainly the devil does not grieve. But God grieves. Christ in his love joins humanity as "a man of sorrows, acquainted with deepest grief" (Is 53:3 NLT). The Logos of God—the logic of divine love—could not become human and *not* suffer. In other words, there is no possibility of loving the world to salvation without suffering. Jesus could not merely spread love and avoid sharing our sorrows. Adrienne von Speyr explains it this way:

> If God brought his love to earth as pure fire, perhaps he would find a few men who would not yet be completely hardened by sin and would surrender to his fire. But his plan is to save us all. And he cannot do this by transmitting the fire of love from one man to another; he must transform his fire into suffering. But, because he himself is all purity and because nothing in him can be consumed, he takes within himself as the fuel the sin of the world and burns it within himself, in the human nature that the Father has given him; he suffers through each of us.[5]

Consisting of pure love, God is indeed impassible and beyond all suffering *until* he loves that which suffers because of sin and death. Then the God who is love *must* suffer more deeply than any of his creation. Once we understand the love of God in this light, we can look at the suffering of Christ upon the cross and truly call it a love supreme. And as we look at the cross, we must not imagine that the suffering of the crucifixion is restricted to the incarnate Son.

Sergius Bulgakov writes, "In the human crucifixion of the Son and the divine co-crucifixion of the Father, love itself is co-crucified." Bulgakov then goes on to identify co-crucified love as the Holy Spirit—the "love uniting the Son with the Father."[6] The Son assumes flesh on behalf of the Trinity and bears wounds in his flesh, but the woundedness is experienced in the indivisible union of the Godhead.

Christ is the incarnate Logos that draws all human suffering into the Holy Trinity, where, ultimately, it is transformed into healing. Love suffers and love heals.

For God, to love is to suffer all until all is made well. "By his wounds you have been healed" (1 Pet 2:24). This is Christian hope at its highest apex: that the love of God will suffer until all is made well. This is what Julian of Norwich called the revelation of divine love and what John Coltrane called "A Love Supreme." The mystics intuit it. The theologians explore it. The musicians compose songs to it. And painters depict it.

A popular motif for religious art that emerged during the late medieval and early Renaissance period was to depict the Trinity in the crucifixion scene. One of the more famous examples of this motif is Sandro Botticelli's *Holy Trinity*, completed in 1494 for the altarpiece at the Santa Elisabetta convent in Florence, Italy. In the painting, God the Father is depicted as a man in sorrow holding and leaning over the cross upon which his Son is crucified. Between the grieving Father and the crucified Son hovers the white dove of the Holy Spirit. Surrounding the Trinity are nine cherubs, while standing beside the cross are the saints John the Baptist and Mary Magdalene. What Botticelli has done is unite heaven and earth in the Trinity at the crucifixion. This is theologically brilliant. The cross is the wood between the worlds that reunites heaven and earth.

A few years ago I visited an art museum in Europe that had a collection of crucifixion paintings done in this style. Though most of them tended to be overly sentimental, I marveled at how these painters' vision of the crucifixion was more profound than that of many theologians. Uniting the Trinity with humanity and heaven with earth at the crucifixion is indeed a profound theological vision.

Sergius Bulgakov is one of the theologians who resonates with the Paschal vision of Botticelli and similar artists. In *The Lamb of God* he writes,

The crucifixion of the Son takes place on earth, but it is co-experienced in heaven as well: the entire Holy Trinity is co-crucified with the Son—"God so loved the world." The dogma of the redemption, like all things in Christianity, must be understood in a *trinitarian* manner.[7]

To speak of the entire Holy Trinity as co-crucified with the Son is daring language, to be sure, but it is far more theologically sound than doing violence to the Trinity by positing the Son as an object of the Father's wrath. The cross is the scene of a love supreme, not a scene of divine domestic violence. The cross is nothing other than the ultimate triumph of divine love. When we look upon the cross, we should above all see love. And when we look upon the cross, perhaps we should chant with John Coltrane,

A love supreme.
A love supreme.
A love supreme.
A love supreme.
A love supreme.
A love supreme.
A love supreme.
A love supreme.
A love supreme.
A love supreme.
A love supreme.
A love supreme.
A love supreme.
A love supreme.
A love supreme.
A love supreme.
A love supreme.
A love supreme.
A love supreme.
A love supreme.

7

A GROTESQUE BEAUTY

Beauty demands to be noticed; it speaks to us directly
like the voice of an intimate friend. If there are
people who are indifferent to beauty,
then it is surely because they do not perceive it.

Roger Scruton, *Beauty*

A Russian Orthodox cross icon sits on my writing desk. When writing, I light a candle before the icon. Shaped like a cross, it consists of five scenes from the Passion of Christ. At the top Christ carries his cross; on the crossbeam is the crucifixion; below that, Christ is taken down from the cross; further down is his burial; at the bottom of the cross is the resurrection. Each scene is painted with vibrant colors in exquisite detail. In the five scenes there are twenty-nine people and three angels. A magnifying glass is necessary to fully appreciate the skill of the iconographer. I obtained this work of art from an icon dealer in Bethlehem years ago, and though the price was not outlandish, it is the most expensive piece of art I've ever purchased.

And it is beautiful.

But it can more precisely be described as a beauty emerging from the grotesque. Beauty is difficult to define, but easily recognized. To behold beauty brings us a sense of pleasure, and the pleasure derived from beholding the beautiful is not limited to artistic endeavors. There are acts of love and sacrifice that can properly be described as beautiful. When Mary of Bethany anointed Jesus with costly ointment of pure nard, he said, "She has done a beautiful thing to me" (Mk 14:6 ESV). Beauty can appear in unexpected places.

The cross icon on my desk contains an artistic juxtaposition. The artistic beauty is apparent, but the subject matter is grotesque. In four of the five scenes, the torture and death of crucifixion are portrayed. As in most crucifixes, the beautiful and the grotesque are synthesized in the icon. We are accustomed to seeing beautiful crucifixes in Orthodox, Catholic, and Anglican churches, but this hasn't always been the case. It took a surprisingly long time before images of the cross began to appear in Christian art, and even longer before the grotesque element of crucifixion was portrayed. The cross as a *concept* was ubiquitous in early Christian Scripture, liturgy, and theology. Even the sign of the cross has its origin in antiquity.

Ignatius of Antioch was a first-century Christian writer and a disciple of John the Apostle, and it's from him that we gain the earliest account of the sign of the cross in primitive Christianity. Ignatius writes, "The sign of the cross is a trophy raised against the power of the prince of the world."[1] In the second century the church father Tertullian reveals how thoroughly embedded the sign of the cross was in the daily life of the early Christians when he writes, "At every forward step and movement, at every going in and out, when we put on our clothes and shoes, when we bathe, when we sit at the table, when we light the lamps, when on the couch, on a seat, and in all ordinary actions of life, we trace the sign of the cross on our foreheads."[2]

In the early church the symbolic cross was present in liturgical gesture, but not as an actual image. Paul could say he boasted in the cross (Gal 6:14), but it would be centuries before Christians would dare to use crucifixion in religious imagery. Why? To the pagan mind it was wildly incongruous to even *think* of a cross in religious terms. This is seen in the polemic writings of the second-century Greek philosopher Celsus. In his attack upon the new Christian religion, Celsus writes,

> Everywhere they speak in their writings of the tree of life and of resurrection of the flesh by the tree—I imagine because their master was nailed to a cross and was a carpenter by trade. So that if he happened to be thrown off a cliff, or pushed into a pit, or suffocated by strangling, or if he had been a cobbler or a stonemason or a blacksmith, there would have been a cliff of life above the heavens, or a pit of resurrection, or a rope of immortality, or a blessed stone, or an iron of love, or the holy hide of leather.[3]

In his mockery of Christian faith, what Celsus gets right is the strangeness of the claim that salvation has come into the world through a gruesome death upon a Roman cross. Yet this claim lies at the heart of the Christian gospel. The early church preached the cross, sang about the cross, and made ritual gestures of the cross, but they did not yet *depict* the cross.

As long as crucifixion was still employed in the Roman Empire, depicting the crucifixion of Christ in church art would have been too daring, too graphic, too provocative. Crosses and crucifixes did not appear in church art until the fifth century—one hundred years after crucifixion had been banned in the Roman Empire. Before then Christian faith was depicted in artistic image by an anchor, a fish, a lamb, or a shepherd. And even when crucifixes did appear, Christ was portrayed as a Byzantine emperor wearing a golden crown and a regal robe. He was shown alive and serene, in front of the cross more so than upon it. The cross was the throne of Christ the king, not a tree of agony. It took nearly a thousand years before a suffering Christ became a common motif in crucifixes.

One of the earliest depictions of a suffering Christ upon the cross comes from the tenth century in Germany when Archbishop Gero commissioned a crucifix for the new cathedral in Cologne. Unlike the Byzantine regal crucifixes, Gero's crucifix was to depict Christ as a suffering human. Worshipers would now behold a Savior in the agony of death. Gero's groundbreaking crucifix has been displayed in the Cologne Cathedral for over a thousand years and it continues to attract visitors to this day. Judith Couchman gives a vivid description: "Over six feet tall, the painted wood sculpture features a lifeless Christ still hanging on the cross. Christ's skin sags from holding the body's weight and his stomach bulges. His head hangs down, with the cratered eyes and contorted lips of prolonged suffering."[4] With the *Gero Crucifix* a measure of realism had arrived in the artistic depictions of Christ's death.

Commenting on the medieval turn toward realism represented in the Cologne Cathedral crucifix, art historian Marilyn Stokstad says, "Not a symbolic sacrificial lamb of God, not a Byzantine emperor alive and crowned in front of a cross, not even a young hero, as in some Early Christian or Carolingian images, but a tortured martyr hangs in front of the worshiper."[5] Yet even the *Gero Crucifix* as it has come to be known, has an undeniable artistic beauty to it. The *Gero Crucifix* is an early example of the medieval synthesis of the beautiful and grotesque in depicting Christ crucified—a synthesis that took nearly a thousand years to appear. Yet is this an appropriate move? Should the gruesome death of Christ be depicted in terms of beauty?

"I'm Not Supposed to Like This, but I Do"

Growing up in a Baptist church and then later as a Jesus Movement charismatic, crucifixes were foreign to me. I didn't encounter them regularly until I began visiting European cathedrals and art museums in my thirties. When I first began to visit Catholic cathedrals I would think, *I'm not supposed to like this, but I do.* I was especially drawn to the beautiful artistic depictions of the crucifixion. Yet a protest arose in me: *It wasn't like that. It wasn't beautiful. It was ugly!* And that's true. If we had a journalistic photograph of Jesus of Nazareth crucified at

Golgotha, we might look at it once, regret that we had, and never look at it again. It would be too repulsive. It would be purely grotesque. There would be no beauty in it whatsoever. Roman crucifixion was deliberately ghastly. It was intended to psychologically terrorize a subjugated people. The very word *crucifixion* was not used in polite company. The Romans certainly weren't trying to create art when they crucified their victims.

This raises an important question for us: Have Christian artists made a mistake in portraying the crucifixion of Christ in terms of beauty? Consider Andre Mantegna's *Crucifixion*, completed in 1459 for the altarpiece in the San Zeno Basilica in Verona, Italy. It's perhaps the best example of what I mean by grotesque beauty. The grotesque is present in the painting, seen in the contorted face of Jesus, his lifeless eyes, his pierced hands, feet, and side, the stream of blood on the cross, and the sorrow of Mary as she collapses into the arms of the other grieving women. But the overall impression of the painting is one of undeniable beauty. There's a reason why it has remained on permanent display at the Louvre in Paris since 1798. It *is* an artistic masterpiece. It *is* beautiful. But is this a mistake on the part of Andre Mantegna and the countless other artists who have brought beauty to the crucifixion? I don't believe so.

The role of the artist is not that of a journalist. The role of the journalist is to document the facts. The role of the artist is to alert us to what we may have missed. Art takes us deeper than the facts. Art moves us beyond the sterile realm of raw data into the passionate world of subjective experience. Think of Vincent van Gogh's *Starry Night*, widely regarded as his masterpiece. Its swirling stars and fantastic colors of blue and yellow make it one of the most recognized paintings in the world.

But does it accurately depict a starry night? When you look up at the stars does it factually look like what Van Gogh has placed on his canvas? Of course not. Van Gogh is not an astronomer; he's an artist. Van Gogh is trying to wake us up to the beauty we so easily overlook.

In *Starry Night*, Van Gogh is shouting at us. *Wake up! Pay attention! There's beauty all around you! Don't miss it!* What Van Gogh has painted on the canvas is what we should feel in our heart when we behold the mysterious grandeur of the cosmos as seen on a starry night.

And this is precisely why the crucifixion portrayed with beauty is such a profound theological insight. Of course the crucifixion was ugly—nailing a naked man to a tree to hang there until he's dead is horrifyingly ugly. But that's not all that is present at the crucifixion of Christ. There is also a beauty most sublime. If all we see in the crucifixion of Jesus of Nazareth is the raw data of a Galilean Jew executed by the Roman Empire under Pontius Pilate, we have failed to understand it. What Van Gogh was doing with *Starry Night* is what Mantegna was doing with *Crucifixion*. At the cross we find the ugliness of human sin, but we also find the beauty of divine love—the beauty that saves the world. That in Mantegna's *Crucifixion* the grotesque is ultimately overwhelmed by the beautiful is not just an artistic move; it is fundamentally a theological move. Only the *theological* beauty of the cross makes the *artistic* beauty of Mantegna's *Crucifixion* possible.

The transformation of the Roman cross from an abhorrent symbol of death into a beautiful symbol of love is a testament to the redeeming power of Christ. If the cross can be saved, the world can be saved. If crucifixion can be made beautiful, all things can be made beautiful. The hope we have for the healing of a world marred by sin and death is that God makes all things beautiful in his time (Eccles 3:11). When artists create beautiful crucifixes, they are not only calling our attention to the beauty of God's redeeming love, they are also depicting our eschatological hope.

Florence, Italy, is the birthplace of Renaissance art. It's the home of Michelangelo's *David*, Botticelli's *Venus*, and Brunelleschi's Duomo. But my favorite art in Florence are the frescos at the San Marco monastery. Between 1439 and 1444, the Dominican brother and painter Fra Angelico covered the walls of the monastery with scores of gorgeous frescos, most of which are scenes from the life of Christ.

Among them are many crucifixion scenes. My favorite is placed above the entryway to a dining hall. Set against an azure blue background Christ hangs in serene death upon the cross with small rivulets of blood trickling from his wounds. Along with a delicate crown of thorns, the head of Christ is surrounded by a bronze and red cross halo. There is even the hint of a smile upon the lips of Jesus—a smile as enigmatic as that of Mona Lisa.

The grotesque is almost entirely eclipsed by the beauty Fra Angelico has created. The fresco radiates with peace. I'm certain that Fra Angelico's frescos contain soul-healing properties. I'm not sure I can explain *how* a fresco of Christ crucified can bring healing to the soul, but I know it is so. Art has the capacity to be a medium between the material and mystical worlds. The very best Christian art (and here I am thinking of Orthodox icons and Catholic crucifixes) can be sacramental. And if our churches can learn to enact the beauty of Christ crucified and thereby become pavilions of peace instead of culture-war barracks, we can begin to recover our swiftly diminishing relevance.

THE TRUE, THE GOOD, AND THE BEAUTIFUL

The Greek philosophers Plato and Plotinus spoke of the true, the good, and the beautiful as ultimate values—sometimes referred to today as the transcendentals. By doing so, Plato and Plotinus meant that these attributes are self-justifying; they need serve no other end. The true is desired because it is true. The good is desired because it is good. The beautiful is desired because it is beautiful. A life lived in accord with the true, the good, and the beautiful is a life well-lived.

Over time the transcendentals of Plato and Plotinus began to inform Christian theology. The true, the good, and the beautiful are ultimate values because they are attributes of God. God is the true, the good, and the beautiful in ultimate perfection. Thus the true, the good, and (to a lesser extent) the beautiful were given their own categories in Christian thought.

Christian apologetics is the defense of the truth of Christ. Christian ethics is the attempt to define the good in the light of Christ. Christian apologetics and ethics have a long and venerable tradition in the history of the church. But what about Christian aesthetics—the formation of beauty as revealed in Christ? There have been times when the church has placed a high value on beauty, but at other times (especially in modernity) the church has tended to dismiss beauty as mere adornment. Much of the modern church regards beauty as an optional accoutrement rather than an ultimate value. This is a mistake that needs to be corrected, because in our present moment beauty may be the best way forward in our witness to the world.

Christian apologetics done well and not at the hands of fundamentalist pop apologists is a valid exercise that will always have its place. Christian ethics is ever an ongoing project that cannot be abandoned. Nevertheless, we live in a time when a post-Christian secular culture is deeply suspicious of any claim regarding ultimate truth or a superior ethic—especially when made by the church. If the church in the secular West takes its stand in the marketplace of ideas by announcing, "We have ultimate truth, we know what's good for you, and we meet at ten o'clock on Sunday morning," the response will mostly be somewhere between shoulder-shrugging indifference and outright scorn. The avenues of truth and goodness may, for now, be closed to the traffic of evangelism.

But what about beauty? What if evangelism could not be easily dismissed as petulant argument or puritanical moralism because it came by the way of aesthetics? Beauty has a way of sneaking past our defenses. As Miguel de Cervantes observed in *Don Quixote*, "It is the prerogative and charm of beauty to win hearts."[6] If in our witness to the world we can set forth the incomparable beauty of Christ, and if we can learn to live beautiful lives in reflection of Christ, hearts can be won, even in a milieu of skepticism. It's through beauty that we fall in love, not through reason or argument. The hope for evangelism in the post-Christian West of the twenty-first century is to trust in the beauty of Christ to win hearts. Let us tell our beautiful story and attempt to live beautiful lives. In evaluating what we do in our churches, we are accustomed to asking two questions: Is it true? Is it good? But now we need to ask, and perhaps prioritize a third question: Is it beautiful?

But what constitutes the beautiful? In whatever way we define beauty it has something to do with form and shape. Whether it's painting or poem, sculpture or song, novel or film, architecture or dance, *form* is central to the achievement of beauty. The skillful arrangement of color, word, stone, music, plot, structure, or movement into that which is aesthetically pleasing is what constitutes beauty. And what is the form of Christian beauty? The answer should be obvious—the *cruciform*. Christ upon the cross, arms outstretched in proffered embrace, forgiving the world—this is the heart of Christian aesthetics. This is the beauty of Christ that Christians are called to emulate.

The cruciform is to be our posture within the world. We are to be present in society, not with the clenched fist of anger, not with the wagging finger of shame, not with the pointing finger of accusation, but with arms outstretched in imitation of our crucified Lord. When we become angry and arrogant accusers, we become ugly. We take on the hideous form of the satan. But when we enact cruciform love, when we "put on the Lord Jesus Christ" (Rom 13:14), we begin to reflect his beauty into the world. To the extent that our posture is cruciform is the extent to which we possess the attractive nature of Christ.

Near the end of my morning prayers, I petition the crucified Christ to clothe me in his spirit of love so that I may be present in the world, not with a clenched fist, not with a wagging or pointing finger, but with the outstretched arms of Christian love. Often as I pray this prayer, I look upon a Byzantine crucifixion icon and imitate the posture of the crucified one. My hope in this daily prayer is that I can carry a small bit of the cruciform beauty of Christ into the world.

Lord Jesus Christ, you stretched out your arms of love on the hard wood of the cross that everyone might come within the reach of your saving embrace: So clothe us in your Spirit that we, reaching forth our hands in love, may bring those who do not know you to the knowledge and love of you; for the honor of your name. Amen.[7]

8

WHAT IS TRUTH?

At the deepest level all hearers of the truth are the same hearer, and when I try to picture him or her, what I picture is the one who is famous for having asked to hear, who took a long drag on his cigarette and through narrowed eyes asked, "What is truth?"

FREDERICK BUECHNER, *TELLING THE TRUTH*

THE NICENE CREED MENTIONS three historical figures—Jesus Christ, the Virgin Mary, and Pontius Pilate. The appearance of Jesus and Mary is obvious, but that of Pontius Pilate is startling. Unexpected as he may be, there he is, for in the creed we confess that Jesus "was crucified under Pontius Pilate." What this line does is establish the life and death of Jesus in a particular historical context.

Christianity doesn't float above history as a timeless abstract. It was born in Judea in the fourth decade of the first century during Roman occupation. Pontius Pilate was the fifth Roman procurator of Judea, holding office from AD 26–36 during the reign of Tiberius Caesar. History has given us scant information on Pilate, but we know he came from a plebian family in Rome that had risen to some prominence through dogged service in the Roman equestrian legions. History also suggests that though Pilate was an effective ruler, he could be particularly cruel to those who resisted Roman rule. Though what we know about Pilate is limited to the gospels and a few lines from Roman historians, the governor who presided over the trial of Jesus of Nazareth has captivated the literary imagination of many a writer.

PILATE IN THE LITERARY IMAGINATION

In his wonderful little book *Telling the Truth: The Gospel as Tragedy, Comedy, and Fairy Tale*, Frederick Buechner imagines Pontius Pilate with comical anachronisms. He is a middle-aged man trying to hold on to his governorship until he can retire to a villa back in Italy and enjoy his evening martinis. The governor has high cholesterol and a three-pack-a-day cigarette habit he's trying to quit. His wife suffers from troubling dreams and is currently seeing an analyst. Early on a Friday morning he's summoned out of bed to hear a case brought against a Galilean Jew accused of capital crimes. Pilate is still in his pajamas. A phone call comes through from his wife, crying and upset by yet another of her troubling dreams. The accused Galilean is brought into Pilate's office. He's clearly been roughed up by the police. His upper lip is puffed out and one eye is swollen shut. Pilate begins his interrogation.

> "So you're the king of the Jews," he says. "The head Jew," because there hasn't been one of them yet who hasn't made that his claim—David come back to give Judea back to the Jews. The man says, "It's not this world I'm king of," but his accent is so thick that Pilate hardly gets it, the accent together with what they've done to his upper lip. As if his mouth is full of stones, he says, "I've come to bear witness to the truth," and at that the procurator of Judea takes such a deep drag on his filter tip that his head swims and for a moment he's afraid he may faint. . . . He says, "What is truth?" and by way of answer, the man with the split lip doesn't say a blessed thing.[1]

Imagining Pontius Pilate as a chain-smoking bureaucrat with a troubled marriage, Frederick Buechner succeeds in making Pilate more, not less, real as a historical figure. Pilate condemns Christ to death not as an arch-villain but as a career politician.

The twentieth-century Russian writer Mikhail Bulgakov does something similar in his clandestinely written and posthumously published novel *The Master and Margarita*, which is set in both Moscow in the 1930s under the rule of Joseph Stalin and in Jerusalem under the governorship of Pontius Pilate. In Bulgakov's telling of the story, Pontius Pilate is a cruel man who suffers from chronic migraine headaches and loves only his dog. After his arrest, Jesus explains to Pilate that all earthly power is a form of violence exercised over people, but that he has come to bear witness to the kingdom of truth—heaven's alternative to violent power. Bulgakov's Pilate answers back, "There has never been, nor yet shall be a greater and more perfect government in this world than the rule of the emperor Tiberius!"[2]

Pilate than asks Jesus if the kingdom of truth will ever come. When Jesus says it will, Pilate erupts,

> "It will never come!" Pilate suddenly shouted in a voice so terrible that Yeshua staggered back. Many years ago in the Valley of the Virgins Pilate had shouted in that same voice to his horsemen: "Cut them down! Cut them down!" . . . A spasm distorted Pilate's face as he turned his bloodshot eyes on Yeshua and said: "Do you imagine, you miserable creature, that a Roman Procurator could release a man who has said what you have said to me? Oh gods, oh gods! Or do you think I'm prepared to take your place? I don't believe in your ideas!"[3]

Frederick Buechner and Mikhail Bulgakov are just two of the many writers who have worked with Pontius Pilate as a literary character. The lure Pilate has upon literary imaginations surely has to do with his almost inconceivable role in history. This is the man who judged and condemned Jesus Christ to death . . . and then tried to wash his hands of the whole affair. The drama inherent in a scenario where God is put on trial and judged by a provincial governor guarantees that Pontius Pilate will always have a unique place in artistic imagination. In medieval passion plays and Renaissance art, in novels like *The Master and Margarita* and theatrical productions like *Jesus Christ Superstar*, Pontius Pilate is endlessly dramatized. Still, the drama we find in John's gospel as Pilate tries and condemns Jesus remains, in my mind, unsurpassed.

CHRIST ON TRIAL

Having been condemned to death in a late-night trial by the Sanhedrin, the ruling religious council of Jerusalem, Jesus is brought early the next morning to the Roman governor, who alone has the authority to carry out a death sentence. The acrimony between Caiaphas, the Jewish high priest, and Pilate, the Roman governor, is never far below the surface. Along with King Herod, these three men are the powerbrokers in Jerusalem, constantly vying with one another for leverage. Pilate is clearly not interested in getting involved with what he views as the arcane religious squabbles of the Jewish people he governs, but Caiaphas will not be put off. Pilate agrees to hear the case and Jesus is brought bound into the governor's headquarters.

Pilate begins his interrogation of Jesus with one inquiry: "Are you the King of the Jews?" (Jn 18:33). This the only question that matters to Pilate. The Jews can have their religion, but everything political belongs to Rome. If this itinerant Galilean preacher claims only to be a prophet, Pilate doesn't care. But if he claims to be a king, there's going to be a problem. Kingship is bestowed by the Roman emperor. To claim it for oneself is rebellion against Caesar. Anyone making a messianic claim to the throne of David is subject to death by crucifixion. Every Roman governor of the troublesome province of Judea encountered these would-be messiahs. And they were always crucified. So Pilate's question is simple and direct.

Jesus' response is also direct, but not so simple: "My kingdom does not belong to this world. If my kingdom belonged to this world, my followers would be fighting to keep me from being handed over to the Judeans.[4] But as it is, my kingdom is not from here" (Jn 18:36). There's a good deal of political theology packed into Jesus' three-sentence reply to Pilate's question. Yes, Jesus is a king, but his kingdom is not something Pilate can easily recognize. The kingdom of Christ is *for* this world, but it's not *from* this world. This world is the one founded by Cain through the slaughter of brother called other and enemy—it's the realpolitik world that Tiberius Caesar sits atop of and that Pontius Pilate benefits from.

The kingdom that Jesus brings into the world is not from Caesar's world of violent power. Jesus was never going to raise an army to establish the kingdom of God. He plainly tells Pilate this: "If my kingdom were from this world, my followers would be fighting." From this simple clarification that Jesus gave Pilate we should be able to understand that if a political arrangement is established through the violent power of war, it's not the kingdom of Christ. Thus the crusades that were launched eleven centuries after Jesus told Pilate that his followers do not fight were the most brazen repudiation of Jesus' teachings imaginable. The crusades were antichrist in every sense of the word.

Pilate's follow-up question is again simple and direct: "So you are a king?" (Jn 18:37). Jesus responds, "You say that I am a king. For this I was born, and for this I came into the world, to testify to the truth. Everyone who belongs to the truth listens to my voice" (Jn 18:37). Jesus doesn't give a simple yes to Pilate's question because Jesus is not the kind of king that Pilate is familiar with. He is nothing like the Emperor Tiberius or King Herod. Their kind of kingship, based upon violent domination, is a deep distortion of the human vocation to bear the image of God. Jesus tells Pilate that his mission is to come into a world of lies and testify to the truth—the truth of what God is like and what humans are called to be. Pilate's cynical reply is legendary: "What is truth?" (Jn 18:38).

Pilate didn't wait for an answer. He left the room, and after further negotiations with members of the Sanhedrin, he ordered Jesus to be flogged. Roman scourging was a brutal and sometimes lethal ordeal that was inflicted upon those condemned to crucifixion. After the soldiers in the Antonia Fortress scourged Jesus, they mocked him as a failed messiah. Donning him with a purple robe and a crown of thorns, they jeered, "Hail, King of the Jews!" (Jn 19:3), and struck him in the face. After the requisite flogging of a condemned man and the gratuitous humiliation at the hands of Roman soldiers, Pilate presented Jesus, still wearing the purple robe and crown of thorns, to the chief priests with the famous words, *Ecce homo!* "Behold the man!" (Jn 19:5 KJV).

The pitiful sight of a bruised and bloodied man wearing a crown of thorns elicits no pity on the part of the chief priests and the temple police as they shout at Pilate, "Crucify him! Crucify him!" (Jn 19:6). When Pilate continues to press the Sanhedrin for a reason why they want this seemingly harmless man crucified, they answer, "Because he has claimed to be the Son of God" (Jn 19:7). For a polytheist like Pilate, the possibility that this Galilean miracle worker might be the son of some god was a troubling notion. Pilate had enough pagan superstition to make him wary. Crucifying a son of one of the Greco-Roman gods was not something Pilate wanted to get involved with. Again Pilate takes Jesus into his private headquarters, and this time his question is different: "Where are you from?" (Jn 19:9). But Jesus gives no answer. Now Pilate's fear gives way to anger: "Do you refuse to speak to me? Do you not know that I have power to release you, and power to crucify you?" (Jn 19:10). And there it is! Pilate has answered his own question. What is truth? For Pilate the truth is nothing but power—especially the power to kill.

Pilate's truth is the diabolical lie Cain was unable to overcome. God warned Cain about the dark intentions already looming in his heart regarding his brother Abel. "Sin is lurking at the door; its desire is for you, but you must master it" (Gen 4:7). Alas, Cain did not master the sin lurking at his door and the founder of the first city gave us the world where the mighty are their brother's conqueror, not their brother's keeper.

Pilate's truth is the lie that the world can only be arranged as a winner-take-all blood sport. Pilate's truth is the lie that ruling the world through lethal power is noble and just. For Pilate the Roman cross is truth. Caesar sits atop the world because he commands the Roman legions and their capacity to inflict lethal violence. This is the only truth Pilate knows: the world is ruled by those who have the greatest capacity to kill—be it by Roman legions or by nuclear arsenals. Those who rule the world as it is are convinced this is the way the world must be. But it's all a lie. Jesus came into the world to bear witness to the truth because the truth had been buried under a mountain of lies . . . and bodies.

In his crucifixion Jesus became the mirror by which the world could see the truth about itself. When we look at the cross, we see the truth that we are not a world of righteousness and justice; we are a world that kills the innocent for the sake of power. And knowing the truth can be a pathway to freedom from our self-deception. As Jesus told a crowd preparing to stone him in the temple: "When you have lifted up the Son of Man on the cross, then you will understand that I AM he. . . . And you will know the truth and the truth will set you free" (Jn 8:28, 32 NLT).

KINGSHIP REIMAGINED

In the end Pontius Pilate was little more than a pawn in a game too big for him to understand. An evil let loose long ago had swept an ambitious pleb from Italy into a series of fateful events that led to the moment when he would ask Jesus, "What is truth?"—and then condemn him to death. The pagan governor did not have the capacity to imagine a world that was not dominated by brute force. But the chief priests should have known better. After all, they had the Hebrew prophetic tradition to draw upon. Prophets like Isaiah and Micah imagined a world where swords are turned into plowshares and spears into pruning hooks. Today we might imagine a world where tanks are turned into tractors and missile silos are converted to grain silos—a world where agriculture is advanced and the military industrial complex is abandoned.

The Hebrew prophets anticipated a day when the God of shalom would become king through his anointed Messiah. The reign of the messianic king would be established not by war, but in peace. Five centuries before Jesus' triumphal entry into Jerusalem the prophet Zechariah foresaw it like this:

> Rejoice greatly, O daughter Zion!
> > Shout aloud, O daughter of Jerusalem!
> See, your king comes to you;
> > triumphant and victorious is he,
> humble and riding on a donkey,
> > on a colt, the foal of a donkey.
> He will cut off the chariot from Ephraim
> > and the war horse from Jerusalem;
> and the battle bow shall be cut off,
> > and he shall command peace to the nations;
> his dominion shall be from sea to sea,
> > and from the River to the ends of the earth. (Zech 9:9-10)

Five days before the Sanhedrin condemned Jesus and handed him over to Pontius Pilate, Jesus fulfilled Zechariah's prophecy as he rode a donkey into Jerusalem amid waving palm branches and shouts of "Hosanna! Blessed is the one who comes in the name of the Lord—the King of Israel!" (Jn 12:13). Now the long-awaited messianic king stands before Pilate and the chief priests wearing a crown of thorns.

But instead of recognizing their king, they reject him, as they tell Pilate, "We have no king but Caesar" (Jn 19:15). This is the ultimate betrayal of all that Moses and the prophets stood for. But it was also a rare moment of honesty.

In telling Pilate they had no king but Caesar, the chief priests told the truth. For all their pretense of holding faith in the Torah and the God of Israel, they too believed exactly what the pagan governor believed: that the only truth that matters is that the world is run by those who have the greatest power to kill. They would certainly give lip service to the prophetic promise that Messiah would someday come and establish a kingdom of peace, but they forestalled it with a simple rhetorical trick of three words: but not now. Caiaphas and his cronies would say, "Oh, yes, someday Messiah will come as the Prince of Peace and establish God's kingdom of shalom, but not now. For now, we must live by the sword. For now, we have no king but Caesar." Then the chief priests played their ultimate trump card: "If you release this man, you are no 'friend of Caesar.'[5] Anyone who declares himself a king is a rebel against Caesar" (Jn 19:12 NLT). This is when Pilate knew he had no choice but to acquiesce to the crowd.

But lest Christians feel superior to the chief priests who rejected Jesus as king, haven't millions of Christians since the time of Constantine done the same thing when we kick the eschatological can down the road by saying that someday the Messiah's peaceable kingdom will come, but not now? When we refuse to live as if the Prince of Peace is King of kings and Lord of lords *right now*, aren't we, too, essentially saying, "We have no king but Caesar"? When we do this, we continue to mistake truth for the lie that the way the world stands is the way the world must be. No! Jesus died to do nothing less than re-found the world. This is how Jesus understood the meaning of his death—a theme that will be explored in the next chapter.

The trial in the Antonia Fortress ends with Pontius Pilate condemning Jesus Christ to be crucified. Pilate then washed his hands and asserted his innocence. Of course, he's not innocent. Wash his hands though he may, like Lady Macbeth, he cannot remove the damned spot of his guilt. Pilate has entered an infamy from which only the saving grace of Christ can rescue him. And therein lies Pilate's hope . . . and ours too. Pilate was not a monstrosity. He was a man fated to represent the world that most of us are all too comfortable with. As Miroslav Volf says, "Pilate deserves our sympathies, not because he was a good though tragically mistaken man, but because we are not much better. We may believe in Jesus, but we do not believe in his ideas, at least not his ideas about violence, truth, and justice."[6]

9

HOW JESUS UNDERSTOOD
HIS DEATH

The cross is the place where the decisive battle between Christ and sin took place, where the powers of Satan brought all their strength to attack, and where they were defeated.

LESSLIE NEWBIGIN, *SIN AND SALVATION*

FOLLOWING SIMON PETER'S CONFESSION that Jesus was the Messiah, Jesus began to speak privately to his disciples about his impending fate. Matthew says, "From that time on, Jesus began to show his disciples that he must go to Jerusalem and undergo great suffering at the hands of the elders and chief priests and scribes, and be killed and on the third day be raised" (Mt 16:21). Jesus told this to his disciples three times. On these three occasions Jesus doesn't mention crucifixion and he doesn't offer any interpretive meaning of his death. He simply says that he will be killed and raised in Jerusalem. It's not until Jesus reaches Jerusalem that he speaks publicly of his impending death and reveals that his death will be by crucifixion. It's in John's gospel that Jesus first gives an interpretation of what his death will accomplish.

A few days before the Passover, when Jerusalem was filled with throngs of pilgrims and visitors, some Greeks, presumably from the

Decapolis region in Galilee, requested to meet Jesus. They presented their request to Philip and Andrew—the two disciples with Greek names. Upon hearing of their request, Jesus said, "The hour has come for the Son of Man to be glorified" (Jn 12:23). Jesus connects the desire of Greek Gentiles to see him with the glory that will be revealed to the whole world in his death.

That Jesus associates his death with his glorification, not humiliation, is evident when Jesus begins to speak to the crowd of his death and what it will accomplish: "Very truly, I tell you, unless a grain of wheat falls into the earth and dies, it remains just a single grain, but if it dies it bears much fruit" (Jn 12:24). Jesus sees his life as a seed that, when sown in death, will produce multiplication in resurrection—an abundant proliferation of the sons and daughters of God. In baptism we are baptized into the death and resurrection of Christ and become the children of God. The apostle Paul says it this way: "Do you not know that all of us who were baptized into Christ Jesus were baptized into his death? Therefore we were buried with him by baptism into death, so that, just as Christ was raised from the dead by the glory of the Father, so we also might walk in newness of life" (Rom 6:3-4).

In his death and resurrection Christ recapitulates the human race. The human telos is no longer in Adam but in Christ, and thus the human race is destined to be brought into union with God. For Paul, union with God is the final culmination of salvation. This recapitulation of humanity in Christ is Paul's ultimate thesis in his great treatise on resurrection: "For as all die in Adam, so all will be made alive in Christ . . . so that God may be all in all" (1 Cor 15:22, 28). *Theos pas en pas.* God all in all. This is the ultimate accomplishment of salvation, and it is brought about through the death and resurrection of Christ. What Paul sets forth in theological prose, Jesus said poetically in describing his death as a seed that will bear much fruit.

But Jesus doesn't approach his death dispassionately like Socrates calmly drinking the hemlock. Having spoken of his death enigmatically as a grain of wheat falling into the earth, Jesus then says, "Now my soul is troubled. And what should I say: 'Father, save me from this hour'? No, it is for this reason that I have come to this hour" (Jn 12:27). The second-century Gnostic gospels portray Jesus as cavalier and undisturbed in the face of death, but the canonical gospels paint a completely different picture. The Gnostics imagined Jesus as a heavenly spirit eager to shed his earthly embodiment and exhibiting no distress at the prospect of death. But Matthew, Mark, Luke, and John tell a different story—they show us a divine Christ enduring real human suffering.

There's a reason why we speak of the *passion* of Christ and not the *stoicism* of Christ. In his engagement with the Greeks during Passover week, Jesus for the first time spoke of being troubled over his imminent death. Jesus knows that his crucifixion is his exaltation, but his human nature also recoils from it. We are standing on holy ground as we are given a window into the turmoil within the hypostatic union of Christ. The human nature of Christ seeks to escape death and wants to be saved from the awful hour, but the divine nature of Christ knows there is a redemptive reason for his death. This inner turmoil will reach its crescendo in Gethsemane when in agony Jesus throws himself on the ground and prays, "My Father, if it is possible, let this cup pass from me; yet not what I want but what you want" (Mt 26:39).

It's true that John's gospel, which accentuates the divine nature of Christ, does not portray his agony in Gethsemane, but it does show us his troubled soul as he speaks of his death during Passover week in Jerusalem. The human nature of Christ is deeply troubled as he contemplates the hour of his death, but his divine nature knows there is a purpose for it, as he says, "For this *purpose* I have come to this hour" (Jn 12:27 ESV, emphasis added). And what *is* the purpose of his death? Jesus tells us, and it is perhaps the most important passage in the Gospels in revealing how Jesus understood his death: "Now is the judgment of this world; now the ruler of this world will be driven out. And I, when I am lifted up from the earth, will draw all people to myself" (Jn 12:31-32).

At the end of this passage, John comments on Jesus' use of the portentous phrase "lifted up." "He said this to indicate the kind of death he was to die" (Jn 12:33). To be "lifted up" was a polite euphemism for the horror-inducing word *crucifixion.* The crowd of listeners clearly understood that Jesus was speaking of being crucified and were confused. "We have heard from the law that the Messiah remains forever. How can you say that the Son of Man must be lifted up?" (Jn 12:34). This passage is significant because it is only the second time in John's gospel that Jesus has spoken publicly of his death and indicated that it will be by crucifixion. But what is most significant—*enormously significant!*—is that Jesus says his crucifixion will accomplish three things:

1. It will judge the world.

2. It will drive out the ruler of this world.

3. It will draw all people to himself.

We might sum up Jesus' own understanding of his crucifixion by saying he believed it would re-found the world by judging the world, exorcising the world, and drawing the world to himself. Let's examine these three accomplishments of the cross.

THE CROSS JUDGES THE WORLD

The cross is where the world founded by Cain is decisively judged. Cain blamed and killed his brother and then founded civilization by building the first city. We live in the world that Cain built—a world of blame and killing. It's a world organized around an axis of power enforced by violence. But at the cross this world is judged. Jesus Christ was condemned to death under the auspices of two men: Joseph Caiaphas and Pontius Pilate. The high priest and the Roman governor represent two towering human achievements—religion and politics.

We might almost say that the world of social construct is the amalgamation of our religion and politics. Jesus was tried on both religious and political grounds. Using religious criteria Caiaphas convicted Jesus of blasphemy and condemned him to death. Using political criteria Pilate convicted Jesus of sedition and condemned him to crucifixion. The condemnation of Jesus Christ was issued from the gilded sanctuary of religion and from the marbled hall of justice. Anachronistically we might say that church and state in all their pomp and grandeur condemned Christ to death. The sentence handed down had an air of legitimacy on both religious and legal grounds. But this system is about to be weighed in the balance at Golgotha.

The victims of Roman crucifixion were nailed to their cross naked. It was part of the shame and utter degradation of crucifixion. Jesus was no exception. "When the soldiers had crucified Jesus, they took his clothes and divided them into four parts" (Jn 19:23). The sense of shame connected with naked crucifixion is still deeply embedded in our psyche. In religious art a depiction of Christ crucified as entirely naked has far too much realism and thus is almost always avoided. But ultimately, it was not Christ who was stripped and put to shame at the cross, but the rulers of the world.

This is one of Paul's most profound insights into the cross—it was not Christ who was stripped and shamed in crucifixion, but the powers that be. "In this way, he stripped off the spiritual rulers and authorities. He shamed them publicly by his victory over them on the cross" (Col 2:15 NLT, margin). Paul is alluding to the Roman triumph where vanquished foes were paraded naked through the streets of the imperial capital. In other words, the cross stripped the principalities and powers of their cloaks of fictional righteousness and justice and exposed their motives as nothing more than a naked bid for power. Caiaphas and Pilate were not adjudicating religious and political justice in the crucifixion of Jesus of Nazareth, they were trying to hold on to sheer power.

The cross judges a world built around an axis of religious and political power enforced by violence as demonic. In the light of the cross, clerical vestments and judicial robes cannot hide the shame of using religion and politics for personal power. The power mongers of this age claim to have a right to rule because they are righteous and just, but the cross puts their propaganda to shame. In crucifying Jesus Christ, the powers that be were shown to be neither wise nor just, but simply ambitious for power. True justice is not found among those who kill in the name of religion and politics. Those who are wise do not maintain their position of power through lethal violence. Paul says that the foolishness of those who rule the world in this manner was revealed at the cross. "None of the rulers of this age understood, for if they had, they would not have crucified the Lord of glory" (1 Cor 2:8). When Christ was lifted up on the cross it once and forever judged a world organized around an axis of power enforced by violence.

THE CROSS EXORCISES THE WORLD

In John's gospel, during the days leading up to his crucifixion, Jesus refers to the "ruler of this world" three times.

"Now the ruler of this world will be driven out" (Jn 12:31).

"The ruler of this world is coming. He has no power over me" (Jn 14:30).

"The ruler of this world has been condemned" (Jn 16:11).

What Jesus calls the *ruler* of this world is what Paul calls the *god* of this world. Speaking of those who rule through underhanded ways, Paul says, "In their case the god of this world has blinded the minds of the unbelievers, to keep them from seeing the light of the gospel of the glory of Christ, who is the image of God" (2 Cor 4:4). The ruler, or god, of this world is clearly identified with Satan—or more accurately the satan (the accuser). Jesus says that when he is lifted up in crucifixion, the satan as the ruler of this world will be driven out.

The phrase "driven out" is used thirty times in the gospels to describe Jesus' ministry of exorcizing demons from afflicted people. Thus Jesus understands the cross to be the place from which the satan is cast out and the world exorcised. The satanic is probably best understood as an enormously complex spiritual-psychic phenomenon of accusation leading to organized violence. More than a metaphor but less than a person, the satan is the phenomenon of accusation and violence that rules the world but is almost never perceived for what it is because the god of this world has blinded our minds. It is the siren song of the satan that draws us into a deadly orbit around an axis of power enforced by violence.

In our spiritual blindness we almost never see the accusation and violence that sustains our institutions as evil. We don't see it as evil because the macabre dance around the maypole of violence achieves seemingly good things—order, stability, security, and government. What we see is honor, courage, and the order violence brings to our society. What we *don't* see is the blood of the innocent victims—and there are always innocent victims. The bodies are always well concealed, and the executioner's face is always well hidden. The accusation and violence that organizes society under the sway of the god of this world is made sacred through myths and anthems, memorials and monuments, holidays and history books. This is how "Satan disguises himself as an angel of light" (2 Cor 11:14).

The famous painting *American Progress* created by John Gast in 1872 is an example of how the satanic is often disguised as an angel of light. In the painting, white settlers in covered wagons, stagecoaches, and trains are led steadily westward by the goddess Columbia, the deified personification of the United States. Columbia, appearing as a voluptuous feminine angel with blond hair and clad in a billowing white robe, travels through the heavens laying telegraph wire behind her as indigenous people and herds of buffalo flee into the darkness from her glorious advance. The message of the painting is that no matter what violence is visited upon the native tribes of the American West, the American empire remains noble, virtuous, and ordained by heaven. All is justified in the name of progress. This is the satanic lie of every empire. This is the god of this world that Jesus drives out by his cross.

Perhaps the opposite of Gast's *American Progress* is *The Two Crowns*—a work from the same period painted by Sir Frank Dicksee. The painting portrays a monarch returning in triumph from a victorious battle. The king is still in his armor, wearing a crown of gold and sitting astride a white stallion while banners fly and women throw flowers. With his left hand the king holds the reins of his warhorse, as his right hand rests on the hilt of his sword. But none of this is what captures the attention of the viewer. Instead, we are drawn to the startled look on the king's face.

As we follow the gaze of the king, we see that he is looking directly at a life-size crucifix. The king with a crown of gold is astonished by the king with a crown of thorns—thus the title of the painting, *The Two Crowns*. The king with a crown of gold has won his kingdom by the power of the sword. But the king with the crown of thorns has won his kingdom by his death upon a cross. The cross shames the pretentious propaganda of empire disseminated by the satan. If we sit long enough with Christ crucified, it will become the place from which the god of this world who rules through accusation and violence is driven out. This is the exorcism we need.

THE CROSS DRAWS THE WORLD

The cross is where Jesus does nothing less than re-found the world. Instead of being organized around an axis of power enforced by violence, the world is reorganized around an axis of love expressed in forgiveness. In the light of the cross the world has been judged. "The darkness is passing away and the true light is already shining" (1 Jn 2:8). From the cross the satan is driven out of the world. "The Son of God was revealed for this purpose: to destroy the works of the devil" (1 Jn 3:8). Jesus' final commentary on the meaning of his crucifixion is his boldest claim. "And I, when I am lifted up from the earth, will draw all people to myself" (Jn 12:32). The world has been held captive in a deadly orbit around the satan, but the cross changes that.

Jesus says that the ultimate result of his crucifixion will be to draw all people to himself. The verb Jesus uses literally means "to drag." Here are a couple of examples of how this verb is used elsewhere in the New Testament:

"Simon Peter went aboard and *dragged* the net to the shore" (Jn 21:11 NLT, emphasis added).

"They seized Paul and Silas and *dragged* them into the marketplace" (Acts 16:19, emphasis added).

Jesus has no doubt about the salvific efficacy of the cross. Ultimately it will drag all people to himself. Does this imply that salvation is forced upon us through overpowering coercion? No, I don't think so. Saving grace can always be resisted by a rebellious will. Rather, I think this has to do with the utter relentlessness of the divine love seen in Christ upon the cross. The gravity of grace is always pulling upon us. At any given moment we can resist the love of God, but, as Psalm 136 says so relentlessly—twenty-six consecutive times—"His steadfast love endures forever."

From the cross of Christ there emanates a tractor beam of steadfast love that pulls upon all people. At any given moment any given person can resist it, but how long can a love that endures *forever* be resisted?

10

ONE RING
TO RULE THEM ALL

One Ring to rule them all, One Ring to find them,
One Ring to bring them all and in the darkness bind them
In the Land of Mordor where the Shadows lie.

J. R. R. TOLKIEN, *THE LORD OF THE RINGS*

J. R. R. TOLKIEN'S *THE LORD OF THE RINGS* is a towering literary achievement. The unassuming Oxford philologist with a genius imagination did nothing less than create an entire mythical world. I've read *The Lord of the Rings* four times and it's probably the most enjoyable and engrossing work of fiction I've ever encountered. I happily lose myself in the sprawling saga as I journey with Frodo Baggins and his friends from Hobbiton to Mordor and back again. This grand epic about the quest of a fellowship to undo the Ring of Power and free the people of Middle-earth from the enslaving shadow of Sauron is a tale that could only have been told by a Christian. I will say it this boldly: Without the gospel story of Jesus Christ, *The Lord of the Rings* could never have been written.

It's true that unlike The Chronicles of Narnia by Tolkien's friend C. S. Lewis, *The Lord of the Rings* is not an overt allegory. Nevertheless, it is a Christian story. As Fleming Rutledge reminds us, "Tolkien himself wrote again and again to his numerous correspondents that he had written a Christian story and that the references were there to be found by those who were looking for them."[1]

In her deep analysis of the Christian themes found in *The Lord of the Rings*, Rutledge identifies two that are the most predominant:

> It is primarily about the unseen Providence of God operating for good through human (and angelic) agents—especially the "little" ones that no one else has noticed.
>
> Secondarily it is about the universal propensity of human beings (and angels) to fall into evil unless they are aided by power from that "unseen but ever-present Person."[2]

The most resonant theme I've found in *The Lord of the Rings* is the nearly irresistible and always corrupting influence the Ring of Power has on all those who try to use it. Ultimately, the Ring could not be used for any good at all. For Middle-earth to be saved from the shadow of the Dark Lord the Ring had to be undone, and that necessarily involved a death—Gollum's fatal plunge with the Ring into the fiery abyss at the Cracks of Doom. What providence accomplished by Gollum's unintended death at Mount Doom is what grace accomplished by Christ's purposeful death at Mount Golgotha. At the cross Jesus Christ undoes coercive power as the means by which the world is to be set right. In the light of the cross the Ring of Power is to be refused, not coveted.

The cross is the antithesis to the Ring of Power, but that does not change the fact that we live in the liminal space of now and not yet, of kingdom come and still awaited. Living between the resurrection and the parousia we must constantly choose between two ways of rectifying the world—the cross of Christ or the Ring of Power. And this is where Tolkien's epic tale of Sauron's "One Ring to rule them all" is so insightful. In *The Lord of the Rings* no one can use the Ring of Power—the capacity to dominate all others—without being corrupted by it. And here we cannot help but remember that famous proverb: "Power tends to corrupt, and absolute power corrupts absolutely."[3]

The great wizard Gandalf understood this and refused to take the Ring when Frodo offered it to him in the Shire at the beginning of the story.

> "You are wise and powerful. Will you take the Ring?"
>
> "No!" cried Gandalf, springing to his feet. "With that power I should have power too great and terrible. And over me the Ring would gain a power still greater and more deadly." His eyes flashed and his face was lit as by a fire within. "Do not tempt me! For I do not wish to become like the Dark Lord himself. Yet the way of the Ring to my heart is by pity, pity for weakness and the desire of strength to do good. Do not tempt me! I dare not take it, not even to keep it safe, unused. The wish to wield it would be too great for my strength."[4]

Gandalf tells Frodo that if he were to take the Ring, his initial motive would be pity and a desire to do good for the weak, but in the end he too would become as corrupted as the Dark Lord Sauron. Thus Gandalf refuses to even touch the Ring.

Later in Lothlórien, when Frodo offers the Ring to the elven queen Galadriel, she too must resist the seductive temptation of power.

> "And now at last it comes. You will give me the Ring freely! In place of the Dark Lord you will set up a Queen. And I shall not be dark, but beautiful and terrible as the Morning and the Night! . . . All shall love me and despair!" . . .
>
> She stood before Frodo seeming now tall beyond measurement, and beautiful beyond enduring, terrible and

worshipful. Then she let her hand fall, and the light faded, and suddenly she laughed again, and lo! she was shrunken: a slender elf-woman, clad in simple white, whose gentle voice was soft and sad.

"I pass the test." she said. "I will diminish, and go into the West, and remain Galadriel."[5]

In refusing the Ring of Power, Galadriel kept her soul—she remained the Lady of the Wood and did not become a female Sauron. In her words of resignation—"I will diminish and remain Galadriel"—we may be reminded of what John the Baptist said when he refused to compete with Jesus for greatness: "He must increase, but I must decrease" (Jn 3:30).

In *The Lord of the Rings* not even the great ones like Gandalf, Galadriel, and Aragorn—especially because they *are* great—will trust themselves to bear the Ring of Power. Only a humble hobbit has even a chance of carrying the Ring to its undoing without becoming corrupted by it. And even Frodo at the end of his long journey was unable to willingly relinquish the Ring of Power. It was finally destroyed only by the intervention of providence. Of all the characters in *The Lord of the Rings*, only Samwise Gamgee, the simple gardener and loyal servant of Frodo Baggins, was able to bear the Ring and willingly relinquish it. In the crucial moment Samwise refused to use the Ring to become "Samwise the Strong, Hero of the Age."

Tolkien's poignant explanation on why Samwise had the capacity to refuse the Ring gives us, perhaps, the most revealing commentary into what *The Lord of the Rings* is all about.

In that hour of trial it was the love of his master that helped him most to hold him firm; but also deep down in him lived still unconquered his plain hobbit-sense: he knew in the core of his heart that he was not large enough to bear such a burden, even if such visions were not a mere cheat to betray him. The one small garden of a free gardener was all his need and due, not a garden swollen to a realm; his own hands to use, not the hands of others to command.[6]

That Samwise Gamgee was content with his garden and didn't lust after an empire is what saved him from the lure of the Ring, and it's what makes him the true hero of *The Lord of the Rings*.

Samwise Gamgee stands in stark contrast with the most tragic character in Tolkien's tale—Saruman, the once wise wizard who in his lust for power became an unwitting servant of the Dark Lord Sauron. And as was the temptation for Gandalf, Saruman was seduced by power from an alleged motive to do good. At the Tower of Orthanc, Saruman attempts to recruit Gandalf as an ally in obtaining and using the Ring of Power.

> He drew himself up and began to declaim, as if he were making a speech long rehearsed. "The Elder Days are gone. The Middle Days are passing. The Younger Days are beginning. The time of the Elves is over, but our time is at hand: the world of Men, which we must rule. But we must have power, power to order all things as we will, for that good that only the Wise can see."[7]

Saruman spoke as a politician, pragmatically appealing to power as the only way to get good things done. Gandalf's reply is curt: "I have heard speeches of this kind before, but only in the mouths of emissaries sent from Mordor to deceive the ignorant."[8] For all his former wisdom, Saruman has become a dupe of the Dark Lord through the seduction of power. Middle-earth would be saved by a sacrificial quest to undo the Ring of Power, not by a calculating attempt to use the Ring of Power. And what was true for Middle-earth at the end of the Third Age is true for we who are passing through the tumultuous decades of the twenty-first century.

THE POISONOUS PROMISE OF POWER

Historian Kristin Kobes Du Mez begins her bestselling book, *Jesus and John Wayne*, with this sentence: "On a bitterly cold day in January 2016, Donald Trump stood on the stage of an auditorium at a small Christian college in Iowa."[9] Du Mez appropriately identifies Donald Trump's speech at Dordt University in Sioux Center, Iowa, as the representative moment when a New York real-estate tycoon and reality TV star captured the hearts and votes of 81 percent of white evangelicals in America. And what did Donald Trump promise in his campaign speech that won over his Christian audience? Precisely this: "Christianity will have power. If I'm there, you're going to have plenty of power."[10]

Saruman's speech to Gandalf at Orthanc and Trump's speech to Christians in Iowa are one and the same. Saruman tells Gandalf, "We must have power," and Trump tells Iowans, "Christianity will have power." As Gandalf said, "I have heard speeches of this kind before." But these speeches get recycled because they work. Trump, ever the pitchman, offered evangelicals political power in exchange for their political support.

Du Mez writes that Trump

claimed that Christianity was "under siege" and urged Christians to band together and assert their power. He promised to lead. He had no doubts about the loyalty of his followers: "I could stand in the middle of Fifth Avenue and shoot somebody and I wouldn't lose any voters," he claimed.[11]

Just as Middle-earth could not be saved, only enslaved, by the Ring of Power, so Christianity cannot save the world by political power; it can only be corrupted by it. Jesus Christ crucified is the everlasting indictment on those who forsake the way of the cross to reach for the ring of political power. The power we are promised by our Lord is the power of the Holy Spirit—the power to love, forgive, and heal. If we try to wield the Ring of Power (or Caesar's sword), it will only corrupt us.

This has been a recurring temptation ever since Constantine offered the church a seat at the table of political power. According to the imperial propaganda of the Christian court historian Eusebius, on the eve of the battle of the Milvian bridge, Constantine saw a vision of a cross with these words: "In this sign you shall conquer." But of course *conquer* is just a sanitized euphemism for *kill*. And to kill in the name of the cross is blasphemy—it is the exact opposite of what the cross means! If the world could be saved by killing the bad guys, God would not have sent his Son. He would have simply sent an army.

When Peter presumed to use the sword for the sake of good in the Garden of Gethsemane, Jesus rebuked him, saying, "Put your sword back into its place; for all who take the sword will die by the sword. Do you think that I cannot appeal to my Father, and he will at once send me more than twelve legions of angels?" (Mt 26:52-53). In that moment of rebuke, Jesus warned Peter, representing the church, that to take the sword is to perish—either by reciprocal violence or by corruption.

The church is given keys, not a sword. Yet when Rome offered the sword of political power to the church by making it the state-sponsored church of the empire in 380, the church willingly embraced the offer of political power. It was probably an inevitable mistake, but it has been our bane ever since. There are always strings attached to Caesar's gifts. For a seat at the table of political privilege and a hand upon the sword of political power, the emperor expects the kind of allegiance that can only lead to compromise.

Christ is ever and always a challenge to the aspirations of empire, but when we get too cozy with Caesar our willingness to take a prophetic stand quickly evaporates. Whether offered by Constantine or Charlemagne or Donald Trump, we keep thinking that political power is a gift instead of realizing that it is a poison that will eventually corrupt us. We are like Boromir who thought the Ring of Power was a gift that could be used without corruption. In his fateful words, I hear the church's recurring justification for the pursuit of political power: "True-hearted Men, they will not be corrupted. . . . And behold! in our hour of need chance brings to light the Ring of Power. It is a gift, I say."[12] But Boromir's lust for the Ring of Power led to his betrayal of the Fellowship.

We don't need Caesar's sword as the Ring of Power, for Jesus has already given the church two powers—the power of forgiveness (the keys of the kingdom) and the power of the Holy Spirit. Prior to his ascension, Jesus told his disciples, "You will receive power when the Holy Spirit has come upon you, and you will be my witnesses [Gk. *martys*]" (Acts 1:8). The Holy Spirit gives the church power to be faithful witness-martyrs to Christ. The church is given the power of co-suffering love, not co-regency with Caesar. The church is not to covet a share in the coercive power of the imperial sword. If Caesar offers it, we must refuse it. We don't need an invitation to Palatine Hill or the White House. Breakfast with Caesar is always too great a temptation. We cannot flirt with political power and not be corrupted by it.

In recent years American evangelicals have thrown away their witness to Jesus Christ as they squander their loyalty on an immoral bully. Robert Jeffress, pastor of Dallas First Baptist Church, expressed evangelical support for the presidency of Donald Trump like this. "I want the meanest, toughest, son-of-a-you-know-what I can find in that role, and I think that's where many evangelicals are."[13] When church leaders are longing for the meanest, toughest, S.O.B. to champion their cause, you know they have already been corrupted by the Ring of Power. The Ring of Power has an owner, and it can never be wielded freely.

Fleming Rutledge explains it like this:

As Bob Dylan once sang, "You gotta serve somebody." Paul puts it this way: "You are slaves of the one whom you obey." Here once again is the apocalyptic viewpoint that Tolkien shares with the New Testament. There are forces at work beyond what we vainly imagine to be our own autonomous wills. Saruman thinks he is free, but he is actually being controlled by Mordor, so all he can do is make small-scale imitations of the immense reality of the Powers of Sin and Death.[14]

SARUMAN IN REAL LIFE

If the church doesn't renounce the Ring of Power as a means of bringing about the purposes of God, it ends up a pawn to merchants and thieves hungry for power. This is the tragedy that we witness in the real-life Saruman who is Patriarch Kirill of Moscow—the head of the Russian Orthodox Church. Rather than acting as an ambassador for the Prince of Peace, in 2022 Patriarch Kirill supplied fawning religious endorsement for Vladmir Putin and his rapacious war upon the innocent people of Ukraine. This betrayal of Christian faith in the name of national allegiance has not gone unnoticed.

On March 16, 2022, three weeks after the Russian invasion of Ukraine, Pope Francis held a video conference with the head of the Russian Orthodox Church. Patriarch Kirill began the conference by reading a twenty-minute prepared statement echoing the war propaganda of Vladimir Putin. A flummoxed and frustrated Pope Francis responded by saying,

> The Church must not use the language of politics, but the language of Jesus. There was a time, even in our Churches, when people spoke of a holy or just war. Today we cannot speak in this manner. A Christian awareness of the importance of peace has developed. Wars are always unjust, since it is the people of God who pay. Our hearts cannot but weep before the children and women killed, along with all the victims of war. War is never the way. The Spirit that unites us asks us as shepherds to help the people who suffer from war.[15]

Despite being told the truth by Pope Francis, Patriarch Kirill remained unrepentant in his unflagging support of Russian's brutal war upon Ukraine. Kirill could only do the bidding of his true master—Vladimir Putin.

After his video conference with the Patriarch of Moscow, Pope Francis told reporters, "The Patriarch cannot transform himself into Putin's altar boy."[16] The sad truth is that Kirill had committed the most craven of betrayals. He had abandoned the cross to reach for the Ring of Power. In the centuries before Constantine, Christians were sometimes martyred for refusing to toss a bit of incense in a censor before an image of Caesar. Their conviction that Jesus Christ alone is Lord and Savior was so absolute that they were willing to become martyrs for their witness. But power corrupts.

On Easter of 2022 Vladimir Putin attended Midnight Mass at Christ the Savior Cathedral in Moscow. The Russian dictator stood near the altar holding a red candle as the Patriarch of Moscow swung a censor of incense—a scene broadcast on Russian television and seen around the world. Upon viewing this bit of religious theater, an Orthodox professor in Canada remarked, "How strange! That the same faith of martyrs who refused to burn incense to the emperor should now do so in its own liturgies."

The philosophy of power appears to be self-evident wisdom. It's the wisdom of Saruman when he says, "We must have power, power to order all things as we will." We think if we can just amass enough power, be it through ballots or bullets, we can rescue the world from evil. But we forget that power to dominate comes from the satanic ruler of this age, not our Lord. The apostle Paul readily admits that the gospel of Christ crucified is foolishness to the unbelieving and to the rulers of this age (see 1 Cor 1:18–2:8). The cross is perceived as the way of salvation only in the light of resurrection. That Patriarch Kirill would chant "Christ is risen" on Easter while still placing faith in Russian armies to bring about good through war, describing the invasion in terms of spiritual warfare, saying, "We have entered into a struggle that is not a physical, but a metaphysical significance,"[17] is the height of hypocrisy. The world is saved by the death and resurrection of Jesus Christ, not by Orthodox soldiers killing Orthodox Christians at the behest of a murderous dictator. A patriarch should know better.

AT THE END OF ALL THINGS

In *The Lord of the Rings*, the salvation of Middle-earth is brought about by the many "deaths" and "resurrections" of the protagonists. Gandalf the Grey falls into the abyss during his battle with the Balrog in the mines of Moria, but later returns as Gandalf the White. Aragon must pass through the Paths of the Dead in order to become King of Gondor. Frodo and Sam are left dying on the slopes of Mount Doom after the Ring is destroyed.

> "I am glad you are here with me," said Frodo. "Here at the end of all things, Sam."
>
> "Yes, I am with you, Master," said Sam, laying Frodo's wounded hand gently to his breast. "And you're with me. And the journey's finished. But after coming all that way I don't want to give up yet. It's not like me, somehow, if you understand."
>
> "Maybe not, Sam," said Frodo; "but it's like things are in the world. Hopes fail. An end comes. We have only a little time to wait now. We are lost in ruin and downfall, and there is no escape."[18]

And so Frodo and Sam await the end on Mount Doom as hot ash falls upon them and rivers of fire draw near. They slip into oblivion at the edge of death. The end has come. But it wasn't the end. *The Eagles are coming!* Eleven days later Sam and Frodo awaken from their comas in soft beds in the Fields of Cormallen and are reunited with Gandalf, whom they had last seen falling into the abyss. Obviously, this is one of Tolkien's plainest allusions to resurrection. But resurrection only comes on the other side of death. Gandalf, Aragorn, Frodo, and Sam all had to die through some fashion of self-sacrifice before they could enjoy the peace of a renewed Middle-earth. Likewise, our world is saved only by the cross of Christ, never by the Ring of Power.

Allow me to close this chapter with the most beautiful and joyful passage in *The Lord of the Rings*. We're told that even Tolkien spilled tears on the page as he wrote this scene.

> Sam lay back, and stared with open mouth, and for a moment, between bewilderment and great joy, he could not answer. At last he gasped: "Gandalf! I thought you were dead! But then I thought I was dead myself. Is everything sad going to come untrue? What's happened to the world?"
>
> "A great Shadow has departed," said Gandalf, and then he laughed, and the sound was like music, or like water in a parched land; and as he listened the thought came to Sam that he had not heard laughter, the pure sound of merriment, for days upon days without count. It fell upon his ears like the echo of all the joys he had ever known. But he himself burst into tears. Then, as a sweet rain will pass down a wind of spring and the sun will shine out the clearer, his tears ceased, and his laughter welled up, and laughing he sprang from his bed.[19]

11

WAR IS OVER
(IF YOU WANT IT)

So this is Christmas
For weak and for strong
(War is over if you want it)
For the rich and the poor ones
The road is so long
(War is over now)

JOHN LENNON, "HAPPY XMAS (WAR IS OVER)"

WE LIVE IN A WORLD WAR HAS MADE. Behind every border is the story of a battle. The lines on the map were first drawn in blood. World history is mostly the record of our wars. We've named our species *Homo sapiens*, "wise man," but we could more aptly name our species *Homo Bellator*, "warrior man." War has been our most defining legacy. Many see this as just the way the world is, resign themselves to it, and hope they're not on the losing side of the next war. To most the possibility of a world free from the horror of war appears to be nothing but an empty flight of fancy.

But the poets are different—their imaginations are less fettered by the propaganda of the powers that be. Poets can imagine the world other than it is. The Hebrew prophets were not social activists or moralizing preachers, but poets who could envision a world not shaped by the machinations of empire. They were irascible poets who often irritated the rich and powerful.

John Lennon was a poet in that kind of tradition. (This may explain President Nixon's strange obsession with John Lennon and his desire to deport him.) In December of 1969, as the Vietnam War raged, John Lennon and Yoko Ono bought billboards and full-page newspaper ads in twelve cities around the world. From New York to Los Angeles, London to Paris, Tokyo to Rome, people saw this message:

WAR IS OVER!
If you want it.
Happy Christmas from John & Yoko

Two years later, in December of 1971, as the war in Vietnam continued, John Lennon released his now famous Christmas carol "Happy Xmas (War Is Over)." As Lennon sings of Christmas wishes, the Harlem Community Children's Choir sings a chorus in the background: "War is over if you want it. War is over now." It's a beautiful song with a hopeful sentiment apropos to Christmas. But it's also easily dismissed by the cynical as the naive poetry of a fanciful dreamer. Yet the poet has done something that too many believers living under the long shadow of Christendom have been unable to do: to connect the coming of Christ with the abolition of war. Yet long before a Beatle made this connection, the church fathers consistently did so.

Here are just a few examples of how early Christian leaders and theologians thought and wrote about war.

We ourselves were well conversant with war, murder, and everything evil, but all of us throughout the whole wide earth have traded in our weapons of war. We have exchanged our swords for plowshares, our spears for farm tools. . . . Now we cultivate the fear of God, justice, kindness, faith, and the expectation of the future given us through the Crucified One. (Justin Martyr, 100–165)

Christians have changed their swords and lances into instruments of peace, and they know not how to fight. (Irenaeus, 130–202)

Above all Christians are not allowed to correct by violence sinful wrongdoings. (Clement of Alexandria, 150–214)

Only without the sword can a Christian wage war: the Lord has abolished the sword. (Tertullian, 160–220)

You cannot demand military service of Christians any more than you can of priests. We do not go forth as soldiers with the Emperor even if he demands this. We have become sons of peace for the sake of Jesus, who is our leader. (Origen, 185–254)

I am a soldier of Christ; it is not possible for me to fight. (Martin of Tours, 315–397)

THE ABOLITION OF WAR

The original church saw Christmas and Calvary as the abolition of war—at least for those who had entered the eschatological kingdom of Christ through baptism. The poet-prophet Isaiah foresaw the coming of Messiah and declared that with his coming, war would be relocated to a barbarous and pagan past.

> He shall judge between the nations
>   and shall arbitrate for many peoples;
> they shall beat their swords into plowshares,
>   and their spears into pruning hooks;
> nation shall not lift up sword against nation,
>   neither shall they learn war any more. (Is 2:4)

When the first Christians read Isaiah's prophecy and saw that the coming of Christ ushers in an era of peace, they simply believed that the time had arrived for all who follow Christ to relinquish their weapons and study war no more. They did not read Isaiah's prophecy of Christ establishing a peaceable kingdom and then say, "But Christ must come a *second time* before we can live as peaceable people." That kind of hermeneutical dodge would never have occurred to them. Their theology of war and peace was simple even if it was demanding: *Jesus Christ is the Prince of Peace who died on the cross refusing to wage war upon his enemies. Now we are called to live as citizens of his peaceable kingdom no matter what the rest of the world does.*

For the early Christians baptism demanded peacemaking and forbid the waging of war. To renounce war was as much an ethical imperative required by their Christian faith as the renunciation of idolatry and fornication. The death and resurrection of Jesus Christ inaugurated a new age of peace that the baptized are called to inhabit now. The baptistry is a time machine that transports the baptized into the fully inaugurated kingdom of Christ. They become those "on whom the ends of the ages have come" (1 Cor 10:11). The baptized do not cling to the disappearing past but embrace the emerging future, which is framed in peace. The church is to be a present witness to the eschatological future of peace that Jesus Christ initiated through his cross.

The apostle Paul describes the church as a new humanity characterized by a peace that was accomplished at the cross. Pay close attention to Paul's theology of peace and its connection with the cross in this dense but rich passage in his epistle to the Ephesians.

> But now in Christ Jesus you who once were far off have been brought near by the blood of Christ. For he is our peace; in his flesh he has made both into one and has broken down the dividing wall, that is, the hostility between us . . . that he might create in himself one new humanity in place of the two, thus making peace, and might reconcile both to God in one body

through the cross, thus putting to death the hostility through
it. (Eph 2:13-16)

According to Paul, hostility was put to death at the cross. The sins of
violent hostility were sinned with violence into the body of Jesus. But
when Jesus absorbed and forgave this violent hostility, war was abol-
ished. By the work of the cross the warring factions of humanity are
to be transformed into one new humanity—a new humanity that is
made a present reality through the church.

If hostile division between Jews and Gentiles is abolished at the
cross, how much more is the hostile division between Christians of
differing nationalities abolished at the cross? At the very least,
baptism should make it impossible for Christians to go to war with
one another! For Paul, the idea that Christians could kill one another
in battle in the name of their national identity would have been in-
conceivable. And yet . . .

THE DARK LEGACY OF CHRISTENDOM

Christians killing Christians in war is the dark legacy of Chris-
tendom. In the fourth century a project was begun with Constantine
to unite the peaceable kingdom of Christ with the imperial mili-
tarism of the Roman/Byzantine Empire. Allegiance to Christ would
now be conflated with allegiance to empire. Baptismal identity
would have to be shared with national identity. With time, this
emerging national identity for Christians grew into the addiction of
religious nationalism, placing the church on a trajectory that resulted
in European Christians killing one another by the millions in two
world wars sixteen centuries later. Despite these disasters, we're still
haunted by the dread specter of Christian nationalism.

The world has witnessed Russian Orthodox soldiers killing
Ukrainian Orthodox Christians at the behest of their would-be czar.
That Constantine is a saint in the Orthodox Church whose icon often
appears on their iconostasis does not help the problem. The sword of

Constantine and successive Christian emperors, kings, czars, presidents, and prime ministers effectively supplanted the cross of Christ, and made possible what was impossible for the early Christians: to wage war . . . even upon one another.

Augustine of Hippo, who wrote a couple of generations after Constantine in an ostensibly Christian empire, departed from the radical peace position of the earlier church fathers by positing the idea of a "just war"—a term coined by Augustine himself. No doubt the Roman emperor was pleased with this new theological development. (Before Augustine's conversion he had been a speechwriter for the emperor.) But even if there can be such a thing as a "just war," the actual implementation of Just War theory has several problems.

First, it requires young soldiers who will wage the war to have access to information and a sophistication in ethics they almost certainly do not have. How many Christian young men are able to perceive the actions of their country as unjust when all critical thought is drowned out by the drums of war? Did young men in Germany in 1939 know the invasion of Poland was unjust? Did young men in America in 2003 know the invasion of Iraq was unjust? Did young men in Russia in 2022 know the invasion of Ukraine was unjust? A few, perhaps, but not many. There are always clever clerics and shrewd theologians who are willing to serve as false prophets for the beast and supply the necessary "justification" for a particular war. This always happens when so-called Christian nations go to war.

The most insurmountable obstacle to the implementation of Just War theory is the age in which we live. Amid modern warfare's long-distance missile strikes and the horrific threat of nuclear and biological weapons, how can the Just War criterion of avoiding civilian deaths be met? Gone are the days when war was confined to battlefields at a safe distance from civilian populations. Today, all war is total war and Just War is just war. It is not those who advocate for peace who are the naive dreamers. If we stubbornly cling to the archaic idea that war is a practical way to rectify the evils of the world, we will eventually have total war between nations deploying their nuclear and biological arsenals. The world cannot be rectified by war, only ruined by it. The madness of modern warfare argues that the only way to save the world is to kill it. In a world after Hiroshima, war is not salvific, it's suicidal.

A PECULIAR PEOPLE OF PEACE

So the world waits for a people who will dare to embody the promise of peace—and the church is called to be that peculiar people. The apostle Peter says, "Since therefore Christ suffered in the flesh, arm yourselves with the same intention" (1 Pet 4:1). How are Christians to be armed? Not with the weapons of this world, but with a willingness to suffer in imitation of Christ.

A theology of peace does not exempt us from a willingness to suffer in the conflict. Christians, like Christ himself, must be willing to die for that which they are unwilling to kill. If we say we believe in Christ, confess Christ, worship Christ, but are unwilling to suffer in Christlikeness, we have rejected the way of the cross and our professed faith is a fallacy. The world is not saved by war, but by the cross. Or we could say it this way: Christ wages war by his cross. It's a war on war. It's the way of co-suffering love that undoes war.

In his crucifixion Christ abolished war. War is over—if we want it. Am I a dreamer? Yes, the kind of dreamer Peter referenced on the day the church was born.

> In the last days it will be, God declares,
>   that I will pour out my Spirit upon all flesh,
>   and your sons and daughters shall prophesy,
>   and your young men shall see visions,
>   and your old men shall dream dreams. (Acts 2:17)

Yes, I am a dreamer, but mostly I am a believer. I believe that the world is saved through Christ and his cross, not through superpowers and their nukes. I believe war was indeed abolished at the cross, and to believe otherwise is to remain in the darkness that dominated the world prior to the dawn of Christ, for indeed, "The darkness is passing away and the true light is already shining" (1 Jn 2:8).

At the end of the passage where Jesus speaks of being lifted up in crucifixion and thus drawing all people to himself (the very opposite of war), he says this: "Believe in the light, so that you may become children of light" (Jn 12:36). There may have been a time when one could innocently believe in war as a way to set the world right, but no more. To believe in the way of modern warfare is to willingly choose to dwell in the outer darkness. "In that place there will be weeping and gnashing of teeth" (Mt 8:12 ESV). War *is* hell.

THE WHITE HORSE RIDER

In asserting that war is abolished at the cross, I am well aware that there are those who will make an appeal to the white horse rider in Revelation as evidence for Jesus himself employing war at the end of the age. After all, we're told, "In righteousness he judges and makes war" (Rev 19:11). Indeed, the one who is faithful and true *does* make war—but how? Through his death upon the cross! This is why the one wearing many crowns and riding on the white horse in the heavens "is clothed in a robe dipped in blood" *before* the battle begins (Rev 19:13). The white horse rider bears a sword, not in his hand as the violent conquerors of this world do, but in his *mouth*. John the Revelator tells us that "his name is called The Word of God" (Rev 19:13). In other words, Christ conquers by shedding his own blood, not by shedding the blood of his enemies. Christ prevails by his word, not by the literal sword of war.

Jesus does not renounce the Sermon on the Mount so that he can imitate Genghis Kahn. Christ wages lamb-like war, not beast-like war. Christ doesn't save the world from the beast by becoming a beast. Those who follow the Lamb conquer the great dragon of evil, "who is called the devil and Satan" (Rev 12:9), not by cruise missiles and carpet bombing, but like this:

They have conquered him by the blood of the Lamb
    and by the word of their testimony,
for they did not cling to life even in the face of death.
    (Rev 12:11)

The vision of the white horse rider waging war from heaven ends with those slain by the Word of God being devoured by the birds of heaven. "And the rest were killed by the sword of the rider on the horse, the sword that came from his mouth, and all the birds were gorged with their flesh" (Rev 19:21). Amen. I count myself among those slain by the Word of God and raised to newness of life. May the fowl of heaven consume my flesh—not my embodiedness, but my carnality.

There is a way to interpret the Apocalypse that is consistent with the life and teaching of Jesus of Nazareth. If we interpret the Christ of the Apocalypse as radically other than the Christ of the Sermon on the Mount, we probably need to reexamine our interpretive method. To literalize the war metaphors of Revelation to turn the Prince of Peace into a divine Rambo is a pernicious interpretation of the text.

Speaking to this point in his commentary on Revelation, Sergius Bulgakov writes,

All these harsh images do not admit of a literal explanation of course, and represent an allegory for spiritual warfare at the utmost level of intensity. This is completely clear, and precludes any other explanation. . . . The images of 19:11–19 must obviously be seen as depicting *spiritual warfare*, since it is completely impossible to interpret this apocalyptic language literally. These images indicate that the combat between Christianity and anti-Christianity is reaching its utmost intensity on both sides. It ends with the greatest victory of Christianity in the world. Nevertheless, it is accompanied not by Christ's coming into the world in a palpable body, but by His spiritually perceptible coming, His active help and participation in the decisive events of history.[1]

We who await the parousia in the midst of "the decisive events of history" fix our eyes upon our Commander-in-Chief—the crucified one. And what does our Commander-in-Chief command of us? "I give you a new commandment, that you love one another. Just as I have loved you, you also should love one another" (Jn 13:34).

The Christ who died on a Roman cross pierced by a Roman spear does not endorse war at Calvary, he abolishes it. It's not the centurion at Calvary who saves the world, but the Galilean hung upon the killing tree. The only redemptive role for the soldier at the foot of the cross is to confess, "Truly this man was God's Son" (Mk 15:39). And once we know the crucified one is the Son of God, we can go about the good work of turning our swords into plowshares and our spears into pruning hooks. We no longer need the weapons of war because war is over.

12

THE SACRIFICE
TO END SACRIFICING

The truth of the human condition is twofold. It is both the truth of the mimetic predicament and the truth of the liberation that comes from revelation of this predicament in the Gospel witness to the crucifixion and resurrection of Christ, which both disclose and overcome the hidden founding murder.

RENÉ GIRARD, *THINGS HIDDEN*
SINCE THE FOUNDATIONS OF THE WORLD

RENÉ NOËL THÉOPHILE GIRARD was born on Christmas day 1923 in Avignon, France. His name means "born on Christmas friend of God" and he went on to become one of the most important thinkers of the twentieth century. His discoveries in the field of philosophical anthropology were as groundbreaking as Einstein's discoveries in the field of astrophysics. Educated in Paris, Girard left France in 1947 to teach literature in the United States where he occupied positions in the universities of Duke, Johns Hopkins, and Stanford until his death in 2015. In 2005 he was elected to "the immortals" of the French Academy. The day I spent with René Girard discussing his theories at his home in Stanford in 2012 is a memory

I will always treasure. He was a towering intellect with a kind and gentle soul.

Girard credits Dostoevsky for putting him on the path that led to his midlife Christian conversion in 1961 at the age of thirty-seven. As he explains,

> Dostoevsky's Christian symbolism was important for me. *Demons* presents Stepan Verkhovensky, whose deathbed conversion is particularly moving, but there is also the end of *Crime and Punishment* and *The Brothers Karamazov*. The old Verkhovensky discovers that he was a fool all the time and turns to the Gospel of Christ. . . . So I began to read the Gospels and the rest of the Bible. And I turned into a Christian.[1]

Girard's interest in Scripture was initially piqued because after reading nearly the entire canon of ancient mythical and religious literature, he saw that the Bible, and particularly the Gospels, were utterly unique. He insists that it is the Jewish and Christian Scriptures alone that clearly reveal the innocence of sacrificial victims who pacify the threat of all-against-all violence arising from mimetic rivalry.

Concerning his work in the field of philosophical anthropology that resulted in over two dozen books, Girard said, "Mine is a search for the anthropology of the Cross."[2] And now I need to briefly summarize René Girard's seminal discovery concerning the origin of human culture and sacrificial victims.

THE SCAPEGOAT MECHANISM

Human beings have very few instincts. We don't instinctively know how to navigate vast distances like geese or how to run from predators mere minutes after being born like gazelle. The instinct we *do* have is that of mimicry. We instinctively imitate those around us. This is how we learn language and, less obviously, how we learn to assign value. We may flatter ourselves that we make our own independent choice when we value something, but this is mostly untrue.

We value what *others* value, especially when it comes to our friends and those whom we admire. This is how a community instills shared values among its members.

It's also why advertisers use celebrities to endorse their products. In purchasing the product endorsed by the celebrity, we are exhibiting what Girard calls mimetic desire—desire based on the urge to imitate a person we admire. Mimetic desire is beneficial if we're talking about instilling shared values, and it's fairly innocuous if we're talking about selling electric razors. But what if the object of desire is not a societal value? What if it is something that cannot be mass produced or shared? For example, what if a man becomes attracted to a woman because his friend is also attracted to the same woman? This is what Girard calls mimetic rivalry, and it carries with it the potential for violent conflict.

This was the problem that plagued *all* early human societies—the threat of mimetic rivalry leading to all-against-all violence. Humans can only survive as part of a society. But how can the society cohere when it's constantly plagued by mimetic rivalry and threat of violence? What Girard's theory reveals is the mechanism by which ancient societies expelled the contagion of mimetic rivalry.

The "miracle" discovered *accidently* and *independently* in *all* primitive human societies by which they were able to avert the threat of all-against-all violence is what Girard calls the scapegoat mechanism. This is what happens when the community focuses their individual anxiety, insecurity, hate, rivalry, and rage upon a single victim, thus temporarily exorcising the contagion of violence and bringing peace to the community. Instead of the community tearing itself apart by uncontrolled violence, sacrificial violence is focused and unleashed upon a single victim. The victim will often, though not always, be relatively defenseless or in some way different from the rest of the community. Once selected, the victim will be accused of crimes that have brought ill-fortune upon the community, such as witchcraft or blasphemy. When the victim is executed, thus achieving a cathartic peace, we might say the victim has borne the sins of the community.

This phenomenon of projecting our own sins upon an accused and vilified victim is known as scapegoating, a term derived from the ancient Hebrew ritual of placing the sins of the congregation upon a goat and driving the goat into the wilderness. The Hebrew word traditionally translated as "scapegoat" in Leviticus 16 is *azazel*, a goat-like demon in Jewish folklore. The ancient Hebrew instinct to connect the scapegoat with the demonic is very insightful. The practice of achieving unity by blaming an innocent victim—what we call scapegoating—is the very essence of the satanic.

Both the Hebrew word *satan* and the Greek word *diabolos* (devil) mean accuser. The primary activity of the satan is to accuse the victim and unite the community around this accusation. In the primordial past the scapegoated person would always be killed by the community. Over time the instinctive and spontaneous killing of a scapegoated victim became ritualized by a priestly class in the form of human sacrifice. The argument that the scapegoat mechanism is the origin of sacrificial religion is compellingly set forth in *Violence and the Sacred*, Girard's landmark analysis of human evil.

In most primitive societies the practice of human sacrifice was eventually mitigated to animal sacrifice—something hinted at in the biblical story of the aborted sacrifice of Isaac in Genesis 22. As modern people we are prone to read the story of the sacrifice of Isaac, or what the Jewish rabbis more accurately call the "binding of Isaac," in an anachronistic manner. We moderns are naturally scandalized by the thought of child sacrifice, but in the ancient Near East the sacrifice of the firstborn was a common enough practice that it wasn't unheard of. When Abraham put down the knife and did *not* sacrifice Isaac, it is a crucial development in religious thought: God does not require human sacrifice. If Abraham is the father of monotheism, we might also see Abraham as the father of the abolition of human sacrifice.

It's important that we notice three essential aspects regarding the scapegoat mechanism. First, the practitioners are unaware that they are practicing what we call scapegoating. Those who are stoning or lynching the victim (whether literally or metaphorically) sincerely believe the accused is guilty of bringing diabolical harm to the community. Those who participate in attacking a scapegoat have no idea that they are participating in a great act of satanic evil. As René Girard says, "To have a scapegoat is not to know that one has one. As soon as the scapegoat is revealed and named as such, it loses its power."[3]

Second, the scapegoat mechanism actually works. That is, it really does bring a cathartic, if temporary, peace into the community. The scapegoat mechanism possesses a dark magic. The unity achieved by a community projecting blame upon a vilified scapegoat, though ethically dubious, is a very real unity. Instead of the community being at one another's throats, the scapegoat takes the blame, thus bringing a sense of relief and comradery. For a time, peace is achieved with the all-against-all finger-pointing set aside as the community harmoniously agrees to place all the blame on the scapegoat. The reason we keep scapegoating is because this dark mechanism actually does produce social cohesion.

The final thing to notice about the scapegoat mechanism is the most important: Though it does produce peace and unity, it does so at the cost of the suffering of an innocent victim. Accusing and sacrificing a scapegoat is the satanic way of organizing a society. We see this in the development of archaic sacrificial religion, and we see it in modern politics, whether partisan national politics or petty office politics. When a group unconsciously but unanimously agrees to pool together their collective anxiety and rage to project it upon a scapegoat, it really does produce peace and unity in the group. But it's also satanic. When a group of adolescent boys on the playground begins to pick on a single boy, it brings an exhilarating comradery to the gang, but at the cost of creating a living hell for the victim.

René Girard discovered that the phenomenon of mimetic rivalry and the scapegoat mechanism to corral the rivalry is found throughout ancient literature from Greek mythology to the great Hindu epics. But he also discovered that the Bible was unique among ancient literature in that it was the first to reveal the *innocence* of the scapegoat. This theme first appears in Job and the Psalms, where the voice of the set-upon scapegoat is no longer silenced. It is more fully developed in the Prophets (especially in Isaiah 53) and set forth in its entirety in the Gospels.

In his crucifixion and resurrection, Jesus Christ is shown to be the perfectly innocent Lamb of God who reveals the relative innocence of all scapegoats. If the sacrifice of a single victim is the foundation of societal unity, Jesus is "the Lamb slain from the foundation of the world" (Rev 13:8 KJV). If turning innocent victims into sacrificial scapegoats is the organizational sin of the world, Jesus is "the Lamb of God who takes away the sin of the world" (Jn 1:29). If sacrificial religion has its dark origins in the scapegoat mechanism of human sacrifice, then Jesus is the sacrifice to end sacrificing. The sacrifice of Jesus does not perpetuate the satanic system of ritual sacrifice but reveals it and ends it.

Girard says it like this:

> If the term *sacrifice* is used for the death of Jesus, it is in a sense absolutely contrary to the archaic sense. Jesus consents to die in order to reveal the lie of blood sacrifices and to render them henceforth impossible. The Christian notion of redemption must be interpreted on the basis of this reversal.[4]

Jesus was a sacrifice in the sense of one laying down his life for another in co-suffering love, but not in the sense of satanic scapegoating, and certainly not in the sense of appeasing a violent and vengeful god. If blood sacrifice involves killing an innocent victim, the sacrificing of Jesus Christ was an act of sinful humanity, not an act of a loving God. "Humankind is never the victim of God; God is always the victim of humankind."[5] The human inclination to hold on to the archaic sacrificing of a scapegoated victim too often distorts our interpretation of the cross.

That is indeed why people are constrained to invent an irrational requirement of sacrifice that absolves them of responsibility. According to this argument, the Father of Jesus is still a God of violence despite what Jesus explicitly says. Indeed he comes to be the God of unequaled violence since he not only requires the blood of the victim who is closest to him, most precious and dear to him, but also envisages taking vengeance upon the whole of humankind for a death that he both required and anticipated.[6]

Violence was visited upon Christ, not at the behest of his Father, but because "violence is unable to bear the presence of a being that owes it nothing."[7] Atonement theories that present the death of Christ as an act of subservient obedience to the archaic order of human sacrifice disregard what John the Elder says about co-suffering love, not murder, being the full expression of divine life. "We know that we have passed from death to life because we love the brothers and sisters. Whoever does not love abides in death. All who hate a brother or sister are murderers, and you know that murderers do not have eternal life abiding in them" (1 Jn 3:14-15).

It should be obvious by now that the cross is not just one thing with a single meaning. "Seventeen centuries ago, Ephrem the Syrian (not exactly your postmodern literary critic) said, 'If there were only one meaning for the words of Scripture, the first interpreter would find it, and all other listeners would have neither the toil nor the pleasure of finding.'"[8] This is especially true in interpreting the meaning of the cross as set forth in Scripture. The cross is not something that can be summed up in one tidy theological formula. The Paschal mystery that "Christ died for our sins in accordance with the scriptures" (1 Cor 15:3) is a multifaceted diamond refracting the light of truth in many and varied ways. The cross is where all that is wrong with humankind and the world we have built is dragged into the light, and where God's forgiveness is

Alexamenus graffito, *Le Crucifix du Palatin*
c. 200

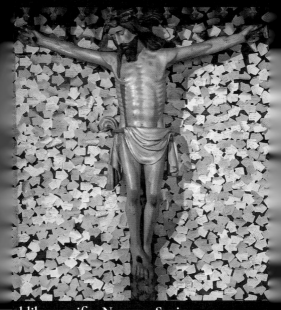

Aldika crucifix, Navarre, Spain

Matthias Grünewald and Nikolaus Hagenauer,
The Isenheim Altarpiece, 1509–1515

Andreas Pavias, The Crucifixion, 15th century

Hieronymus Bosch, *Christ Carrying the Cross*,
1505–1507

Big Love, mosaic in the Golgotha chapel at the
Church of the Holy Sepulchre, Jerusalem

Sandro Botticelli, *Holy Trinity (Pala della Convertite)*, 1491–1494

Andrea Mantegna, *Crucifixion*, 1459

Cross icon

Fra Angelico, Crucifixion fresco, Saint
Dominic Adoring the Crucifixion

Gero Crucifix, Cologne, Germany, 970

Antonio Ciseri, *Ecce Homo*, 1871

Frank Dicksee, *The Two Crowns*, 1900

Ἡ ΚΟΙΜΗϹΙϹ ΤΗϹ ΘΕΟΤΟΚΟΥ

Anastasis fresco depicting the resurrection of Christ, Church of St. Savior in Chora, Istanbul, c. 1320

Ivanka Demchuk, *Resurrection*

offered as a redemptive alternative. Through the revelation of the cross we make the anthropological discovery that Jesus is the sacrifice to end violent sacrificing.

The title "Lamb of God" refers to Jesus as the perfectly innocent scapegoat. Girard explains it like this:

> One might object that the word "scapegoat" never appears in the Gospels, and to this I respond that the word itself is of little importance; all that matters is the reality behind it. There exists, moreover, in the New Testament, an expression applied to Jesus alone that captures everything the word "scapegoat" signifies; the metaphor is very close to the one I use but far superior to it. The expression is "lamb of God," which rids us of the pointless vulgarity of the goat and makes even more visible the innocence of the unjustly sacrificed victim.[9]

Making others bear our blame is one of the foundational sins of the world. In Genesis the world of human society was founded when Cain blamed and killed (sacrificed) his brother Abel. In Revelation Jesus is described as the Lamb slain from the foundation of the world. We might think of it like this: Jesus is the Lamb slain from the foundational sin of the world. Jesus is called the *lamb* of God instead of the *goat* of God to stress his innocence. In his condemnation and crucifixion Jesus re-founds the world by identifying with all the sacrificed Abels and none of the sacrificing Cains. Jesus re-founds the world by sacrificing his own blood to end the foundational sin of sacrificing victims.

Jesus is the innocent lamb/scapegoat who was expelled from the congregation (by execution) *and comes back!* The resurrection of Jesus Christ is the return of the innocent-but-condemned-and-sacrificed scapegoat. John the Revelator says, "I saw a Lamb that looked as if it had been slaughtered, but it was now standing" (Rev 5:6 NLT). Jesus is the innocent scapegoat who comes back from his fatal banishment. And the Lamb comes back, not seeking revenge, but offering forgiveness and showing us the way out of the satanic system that demands more victims. Jesus took all the blame, carried it down into Hades, and left it there. In his resurrection Jesus comes to us, not blaming, but speaking the first word of a new world: "Peace be with you" (Jn 20:21). Jesus has opened the door to a new world where peace can be achieved without projecting blame onto scapegoats. In his crucifixion Jesus dragged the scapegoat mechanism out of the darkness and into the light so that we could see it for what it is and once and for all abandon it.

THE SACRIFICE OF A SINGLE VICTIM

When Jesus arrived in Jerusalem for the final time, the Sanhedrin convened an emergency meeting to address the problem of his increasing popularity. The alarmed Sanhedrin complained, "If we let him go on like this, everyone will believe in him, and the Romans will come and destroy both our holy place and our nation" (Jn 11:48). In response to the threat they perceived in Jesus, the high priest, Caiaphas, plotted a course of action. They would unite the people of Jerusalem against Jesus by accusing him of blasphemy and then sacrifice him in crucifixion. Caiaphas told the council, "You know nothing at all! You do not understand that it is better for you to have one man die for the people than to have the whole nation destroyed" (Jn 11:49-50).

In his address to the Sanhedrin, Caiaphas virtually unveils the scapegoat mechanism to unite and preserve the community by accusing and sacrificing a single victim. But the Evangelist tells us that Caiaphas was saying far more than he knew. "He did not say this on his own, but being the high priest that year he prophesied that Jesus was about to die for the nation, and not for the nation only, but to gather into one the dispersed children of God" (Jn 11:51-52).

From the foundation of the world, human culture has achieved unity by gathering against a sacrificial scapegoat, but the innocence of the scapegoat is always carefully hidden. For the scapegoat mechanism to work its fiendish magic the community must be convinced of the guilt of the sacrificial victim. *He really is a blasphemer! She really is a witch!* But when the satan accused and crucified the innocent one, who was then vindicated by God in resurrection, the diabolical evil of the scapegoat mechanism was revealed.

After the resurrection, Peter, while preaching to the very same people who had cried out for Jesus' crucifixion, said, "You rejected the holy and righteous one and asked to have a murderer given to you, and you killed the author of life, whom God raised from the dead" (Acts 3:14-15). Jesus himself had anticipated this when he told the same people, "You are from your father the devil, and you choose to do your father's desires. He was a murderer from the beginning and does not stand in the truth because there is no truth in him" (Jn 8:44). Jesus tells his accusers under the sway of the satan that they are about to do to him what Cain did to Abel: lie and murder. Jesus is revealing that sacrificial killing does not come from God the Father, it comes from the devil, the father of lies. Yet in his resurrection, Jesus never speaks a word of vengeance, but only of peace.

In his parable of the wicked tenants, Jesus anticipates being killed by the chief priests and scribes, casting himself as the son of the vineyard owner who is murdered by the tenants of the vineyard. Mark tells us that the rulers understood the implication of the parable, adding, "They realized that he had told this parable against them" (Mk 12:12). Jesus concludes the parable by quoting from Psalm 118.

> The stone that the builders rejected,
>   has become the cornerstone;
> this was the Lord's doing,
>   and it is amazing in our eyes. (Mk 12:10-11)

Shortly after the crucifixion and resurrection, Peter and John healed a crippled beggar in the name of Jesus at the Beautiful Gate in the temple and were subsequently arrested for preaching that the resurrection of the dead is found in Jesus. In his defense before the Sanhedrin, Peter made explicit what Jesus had tacitly set forth in the parable of the wicked tenants. "This man is standing before you in good health by the name of Jesus Christ of Nazareth, whom you crucified, whom God raised from the dead. This Jesus is 'the stone that was rejected by you, the builders; it has become the cornerstone'" (Acts 4:10-11).

In his parable Jesus is revealing "what has been hidden since the foundation of the world" (Mt 13:35 ESV). The cornerstone of human civilization has always been a founding murder—Cain's murder of Abel repeated over and over. But with the crucifixion of Jesus something new happened. Jesus was the scapegoat rejected and killed by the builders, but in his resurrection, Jesus becomes the cornerstone of a new world, not one built on sacrificial violence, but one built on universal love. The world is now to be united around the crucified and risen Lamb of God, and the sacrificing of victims is to be forever abandoned.

Simon Peter concluded his sermon to the people in the temple after they had witnessed the healing of the crippled beggar by giving them this invitation.

> And now, brothers and sisters, I know that you acted in ignorance, as did also your rulers. In this way God fulfilled what he had foretold through all the prophets, that his Messiah would suffer. Repent, therefore, and turn to God so that your sins may be wiped out, so that times of refreshing may come from the presence of the Lord and that he may send the Messiah appointed for you, that is, Jesus, who must remain in heaven until the time of universal restoration that God promised long ago through his holy prophets. (Acts 3:17-21)

The way toward universal restoration does not involve uniting in hatred of a common enemy. Achieving unity in a community by vilifying those who are religiously, ethnically, politically, or sexually different from us is forever condemned by the cross. Jesus' death as an accused-but-innocent sacrificial scapegoat ends the ancient satanic practice of sacrificing scapegoats. The blame game is the devil's game. When Jesus is raised he doesn't speak a word of recrimination. Instead he insists we no longer play the devil's game. "'Peace be with you. As the Father has sent me, so I send you.' When he had said this, he breathed on them and said to them, 'Receive the Holy Spirit'" (Jn 20:21-22).

One way to think about the Holy Spirit is to understand that the Spirit of God is the very opposite of the unholy spirit—the spirit of the satan. The unholy spirit is the spirit of accusation. It is the demonic impulse to blame and accuse others. The Holy Spirit is the spirit of advocacy. Jesus spoke of the promise of the Holy Spirit by saying, "I will ask the Father, and he will give you another Advocate, to be with you forever" (Jn 14:16). In his ministry Jesus Christ was always the advocate for the accused. We see this most dramatically in his advocacy for the woman caught in adultery.

When the accusers came under the spell of the satan and turned into a murderous mob, Jesus stood in advocacy with the accused and broke the satanic spell by calling for self-reflection and individual responsibility. "Let anyone among you who is without sin be the first to throw a stone" (Jn 8:7). When Jesus breathes on us, we receive his Spirit, and we are compelled toward advocacy. When we are filled with this Holy Spirit, we will not scapegoat or belong to a lynch mob. In his crucifixion Jesus was the victim of a first-century mob lynching. This lynching of the Son of Man is what we turn to next.

13

THE LYNCHING
OF THE SON OF MAN

They're selling postcards of the hanging

Bob Dylan, "Desolation Row"

Between 1880 and 1940 there were nearly five thousand public lynchings of African Americans by white mobs in the United States. Most occurred in the former Confederate States of the South. These were not clandestine executions but public events, often attended by as many as ten or twenty thousand men, women, and children. Newspapers announced the time and location of the lynching. These gruesome spectacles had a carnival-like atmosphere. They were a repugnant, unabashed celebration of white supremacy. Onlookers would pose for pictures, smiling and pointing at the hanged victim.

The crime of mob-murder was not covered up. Instead postcards were made of the hanging and sold for twenty-five cents. In June of 1915 a Tennessee magazine reporting on the lynching of Thomas Brooks in Fayette County, wrote this:

Hundreds of kodaks clicked all morning at the scene of the lynching. People in automobiles and carriages came from miles

around to view the corpse dangling from the end of a rope. . . .
Picture cards photographers installed a portable printing plant
at the bridge and reaped a harvest selling the postcard showing
a photograph of the lynched Negro.[1]

The lynching of Black victims by white mobs was a manifestation of
the satan as the white community united in accusation and expelled
their fear, insecurity, loathing, and rage upon a single scapegoated
victim. A Black man, or on some two hundred occasions, a Black
woman, was made to bear the sin of white supremacy.

The atmosphere at a public lynching was not foreboding, but full
of jovial comradery as the murderous crowd achieved a cathartic
union through the act of human sacrifice. Under the spell of the satan
the crowd was immune to any sense of guilt, convinced of the
rightness of their actions. They were demon-possessed. The crowd
became the satan. But the cross of Jesus Christ is where the spell of
mob violence and collective killing can and should be broken.

René Girard points out, "When Jesus accepts to die on the Cross he
accepts being one of the innumerable unknown victims upon which
human order has always been based."[2] The only way for the Southern
white mob at a lynching—the vast majority of whom thought them-
selves fine Christians—to be delivered from the demonic possession
of white supremacist hate and murder was to see Jesus in the lynched
Black man, or better yet, to see Jesus *as* a lynched Black man. They
needed a Damascus Road moment where they heard Jesus say,
"Southern Man, Southern Man, why do you lynch me?" They needed
to remember what Jesus said in his parable of the sheep and the goats:
"As you did it to one of the least of these my brothers, you did it to me"
(Mt 25:40 ESV). In 1971 Neil Young sang about it pointedly: "Southern
man, better keep your head / Don't forget what your good book said."[3]

But they did forget because they had been trained to forget. They
had been mistaught in countless revival sermons and nineteenth-
century hymns that the cross is what God inflicted on Jesus in order

to satisfy justice. (As if justice could be satisfied with an unjust murder!) They could only see the cross as what they imagined to be an act of divine justice in the form of violent retribution rather than an *injustice* in the form of the public lynching of a Galilean Jew.

Any atonement theory that blinds us to how Jesus' crucifixion places him in solidarity with every lynched African American is a theory that does not explain the cross, it only obfuscates it. In light of the history of lynching in America, the words of Simon Peter regarding the death of Jesus at the hands of wicked men take on a new resonance: "They put him to death by hanging him on a tree" (Acts 10:39).

THE CROSS AND THE LYNCHING TREE

In his landmark book, *The Cross and the Lynching Tree*, theologian James Cone writes, "The lynching tree is the cross in America. When American Christians realize that they can meet Jesus only in the crucified bodies in our midst, they will encounter the real scandal of the cross."[4] Once we make the connection between the Roman cross and the American lynching tree, we can recover the true horror of what Christ endured. If we can connect the cross with the lynching tree, we can begin to understand the scandalous nature of the message of the cross in the early centuries of the church.

Unfortunately, we are prone to resist making this connection, as Cone observes.

> The lynching tree—so strikingly similar to the cross on Golgotha—should have a prominent place in American images of Jesus' death. But it does not. In fact, the lynching tree has no place in American theological reflections about Jesus' cross or in the proclamation of Christian churches about his Passion. The conspicuous absence of the lynching tree in American theological discourse and preaching is profoundly revealing, especially since the crucifixion was clearly a first-century lynching.[5]

American lynchings in the late nineteenth and early twentieth century were almost entirely inflicted by white southerners upon the Black descendants of slaves, just as Roman crucifixions were most often inflicted upon slaves. Though Jesus was not a Jewish slave, he did die the death of a slave—a fact that the apostle Paul makes explicit in his hymn of the cross.

> Who, though he existed in the form of God,
>> did not regard equality with God
>> as something to be grasped,
> but emptied himself,
>> taking the form of a *slave*,
>> assuming human likeness.
> And being found in appearance as a human,
>> he humbled himself
>> and became obedient to the point of death—
>> *even death on a cross*. (Phil 2:6-8, emphasis added)

The depth of scandal found in God as a Jewish man suffering the slave-death of crucifixion is felt as we imagine God as a Black man suffering the slave-death of lynching. And it was this leap of theological imagination that enabled the African American churches in the Jim Crow South to see their own story in the Bible.

Like the ancient Israelites, they too had been enslaved. Like Joseph, they too were in danger of false accusation and false imprisonment. Like the Hebrew children in the fiery furnace, they too were imperiled by cruel and powerful officials. And like Jesus, they too were in danger of being lynched. The Black experience under white dominance in America gave the African American church a subjective insight into the Jewish experience under Egyptian, Babylonian, and Roman dominance. "The crucifixion of Jesus by the Romans in Jerusalem and the lynching of blacks by whites in the United States are so amazingly similar that one wonders what blocks the American Christian imagination from seeing the connection."[6]

It was the close parallel of the Jewish and African American experiences that had such a profound impact on Dietrich Bonhoeffer while he studied at Union Seminary in New York and worshiped at the Abyssinian Baptist Church in Harlem. Bonhoeffer marveled that he was "increasingly discovering greater religious power and originality among Negroes [and] only heard a genuine proclamation of the gospel from a Negro."[7] It's safe to assume that Dietrich Bonhoeffer would not have become the important theologian that he became had he not learned to see the Jewish Christ through the eyes of African American Christians.

The reality of Hebrew suffering in the Bible paralleled by African American suffering in daily life was reflected upon not only in sermons but also in song. These songs were the spirituals of the church house and the blues of the juke joint. What is Robert Johnson, the most influential bluesman in history, referencing when he sings "Hell Hound on My Trail"? Johnson is cryptically singing about the ever-present danger of a Black man being pursued by a lynch mob or a sheriff's posse in the Mississippi delta.

And these days keep on worryin' me
There's a hell hound on my trail, hell hound on my trail.[8]

STRANGE FRUIT

One of the most important songs in the history of popular American music is the result of a collaboration between a Jewish songwriter and an African American jazz singer. In 1937 Abel Meeropol, a Jewish songwriter in New York, composed "Strange Fruit," a protest song about lynching in the American South. In 1939 it was recorded by Billie Holiday, an African American jazz singer. In 1999 *Time* magazine called Billie Holiday's rendition of "Strange Fruit" the "Best Song of the Century."[9]

Black body swinging in the Southern Breeze,
Strange fruit hanging from the poplar trees.[10]

Written in a minor key, the melody is brooding and melancholy—apropos to its grim lyrics. Billie Holiday summons her considerable talent as a jazz singer in her delivery of the song.

When she performed it live, as she often did, but always reluctantly, she did so with an unmistakable air of anger and contempt. It was a protest song sung by an African American woman who knew the subject matter all too well. Commenting on "Strange Fruit," James Cone says, "It was fitting for a Jew to write this great protest song about 'burning flesh' because the burning of Black bodies on the American landscape prefigured the burning bodies of Jews at Auschwitz and Buchenwald."[11] In some ways, Abel Meeropol and Billie Holiday's song is reminiscent of how Peter spoke of the cross: "He himself bore our sins in his body on the cross" (1 Pet 2:24).

Because we know the gospel story ends in the resurrection and exaltation of Jesus Christ, it can be easy to forget just how shameful his death was. The word *crucifixion* has become connected with glory in a way the word *lynching* has not. Lynching is an ugly word. And as such it is also a powerful word. The way "lynching" sounds to African Americans is how "crucifixion" sounded to people without Roman citizenship in the first century. Imagine the apostle Paul preaching the gospel of the cross in Mississippi in the 1930s. Now take some of his famous sayings about the crucifixion but change the word to lynching and see what happens.

"For I decided to know nothing among you except Jesus Christ and him *lynched*" (1 Cor 2:2).

"I have been *lynched* with Christ" (Gal 2:19).

"May I never boast of anything except the *lynching tree* of our Lord Jesus Christ" (Gal 6:14).

Hearing these verses in this way recovers the scandal of the cross. Perhaps I could push it right to the brink by imagining Paul in Mississippi saying, "We preach Christ lynched, a scandal to Blacks and foolishness to whites" (1 Cor 1:23). That hits hard! As it should. But the jarring connection between the cross and the lynching tree is what the Black church instinctively saw.

> In the mystery of God's revelation, black Christians believed that just knowing that Jesus went through an experience of suffering in a manner similar to theirs gave them faith that God was with them, even suffering on lynching trees, just as God was present with Jesus in the suffering of the cross.[12]

As should be clear by now, the cross has *many* meanings. The cross is the epicenter of grace and forgiveness, *and* it is the ultimate condemnation of the principalities and powers. The cross speaks in many ways.

One way it speaks is to restore the robbed dignity of those set upon by the demonic mob. The cross of Christ restores the dignity of every Black man falsely accused of rape and hung from a lynching tree. The cross of Christ restores the dignity of every woman falsely accused of being a witch and burned at the stake. If we can see Jesus in a lynched Black man in the American South, we can also see Jesus in a woman burned at the stake in Salam, Massachusetts, in the 1690s. These innocent victims of mob hysteria are accorded a retrospective dignity because the Son of God has suffered in solidarity with them. Jesus can and does speak to them saying, "I too suffered just like you. And as my Father raised me up, so I will raise you up."

The satan-impelled mob will not have the last word concerning their victims. In John 5 Jesus reveals that the Father has given the Son of Man all authority to execute the final judgment. Then Jesus says, "Do not be astonished at this, for the hour is coming when all who are in their graves will hear his voice and will come out: those who have done good to the resurrection of life, and those who have done evil to the resurrection of condemnation" (Jn 5:28-29).

THE LYNCHING OF LLOYD WARNER

On November 28, 1933, a white mob of seven thousand people in St. Joseph, Missouri—my city—lynched and burned an eighteen-year-old Black man. His name was Lloyd Warner. He had been falsely accused with what was almost always the accusation that led to lynching—assaulting a white woman. Warner was arrested and placed in the courthouse jail. As word of Warner's "crime" spread throughout the city, thousands gathered at the courthouse where a psychic-satanic maelstrom began to possess the crowd with bloodlust. Around 11:00 p.m. the sheriff surrendered Warner to the mob. The teenager was beaten, choked, and stabbed before being lynched and burned across the street from the courthouse. Some witnesses say he was still alive when he was drenched in gasoline and set on fire.

To further add to the atrocity, the white girl who falsely accused Lloyd Warner later admitted to several newspapers that she "might have gotten the wrong one." I can't imagine the horror! The horror experienced not only by Lloyd Warner but by every Black citizen in St. Joseph.

On November 28, 2013—seventy years later—I went to the site of this lynching. I prayed and confessed this horrible sin on behalf of my city. But the only real comfort I can find is in the conviction that the crucified Son of Man will dispel all darkness by the light of his cross, raise and exonerate Lloyd Warner, and bring his accusers and killers before the judgment seat of Christ.

The cross speaks in many ways, but to those who suffer from an ever-present threat of extra-juridical execution because of their ethnicity, it speaks in a unique way. Regarding how African American Christians have found solace through their faith in the crucified Son of Man, James Cone says,

> Faith that emerged out of the scandal of the cross is not a faith of intellectuals or elites of any sort. This is the faith of abused and scandalized people—the losers and the down and out. It

was this faith that gave blacks the strength and courage to hope, "to keep on keeping on," struggling against the odds, with what Paul Tillich called "the courage to be."[13]

What historians call the "Lynching Era" in America lasted for about sixty years from just after Reconstruction to just before WWII. Thus it would be easy to pretend that white supremacist violence against African Americans has been left in the past. Sadly, this is not so. Lynchings as public spectacles where postcards are sold no longer occur, but the advent of cellphone cameras has made us aware of the systemic sin of unarmed African Americans killed by the police. Eric Garner, Michael Brown, Tamir Rice, Breonna Taylor, and George Floyd are just some of the names we know of African Americans who have died unjustly from police bullets and chokeholds. When Eric Garner and George Floyd gasped, "I can't breathe," it should remind us of the one unjustly executed by the Roman state who gasped, "I thirst."

The cross is many things. One of the revelations of the cross is the divine repudiation of systems that seek to dominate a minority population through lethal force. When the powers that be justify their actions with empty euphemisms like "appropriate use of force," the cross calls them to account. No doubt Pontius Pilate deemed the sentence he passed upon Jesus of Nazareth an "appropriate use of force," but the whole world now knows otherwise. Maybe that's why Pilate's wife had nightmares, and sent word to her husband saying, "Have nothing to do with that innocent man, for today I have suffered a great deal because of a dream about him" (Mt 27:19).

This is a difficult chapter for me to write because I write as a Roman and not as a Jew. I write as a white man and not as an African American. I can only try to gain some sense of the Black experience in white America by listening to the voices of my Black brothers and sisters. So I will yield the closing of this chapter to James Cone and the conclusion of his book *The Cross and the Lynching Tree*.

The lynching tree is a metaphor for white America's crucifixion of black people. It is the window that best reveals the religious meaning of the cross in our land. In this sense, black people are Christ figures, not because they wanted to suffer but because they had no choice. Just as Jesus had no choice about being lynched. The evil forces of the Roman state and of white supremacy in America willed it. Yet, God took the evil of the cross and the lynching tree and transformed them both into the triumphant beauty of the divine. If America has the courage to confront the great sin and ongoing legacy of white supremacy with repentance and reparation, there is hope "beyond tragedy."[14]

14

THE CROSS AND
CAPITAL PUNISHMENT

To take a life when a life has been lost is revenge, not justice.

DESMOND TUTU

WHEN HE CARRIED HIS CROSS through the jeering crowd and endured the ugly shouts of "Crucify him! Crucify him!" Jesus entered into solidarity with all who have been killed through scapegoat sacrificing and mob violence. But ultimately Jesus was executed by the state. It was Pontius Pilate who handed down the sentence of crucifixion. The chief priests told the truth when they said to the governor, "We are not permitted to put anyone to death" (Jn 18:31). Jesus of Nazareth was nailed to the cross at Golgotha because he had been sentenced to death by the Roman governor and the execution was carried out by Roman soldiers. So how does the cross inform us on capital punishment?

In the light of the cross of Christ we should conclude that a practice capable of *committing the greatest act of injustice in time and eternity* must be abandoned! The greatest sin possible, the sin of deicide, the murder of God, was committed through the imposition of capital punishment. If the death penalty can go so wrong that it murders God, a Christian conscience can do nothing other than call for its abolition. In other words, humanity should stop doing that which led to the worst thing humanity has ever done. In his trial before the Sanhedrin, Saint Stephen condemned those who called for Jesus' execution by saying, "You have become his betrayers and murderers" (Acts 7:52). Their response was to execute Stephen by stoning. Another death penalty gone wrong. There is nothing in the New Testament that casts capital punishment in a good light.

What About the Old Testament?

What about the death penalty in the Old Testament? Doesn't a single Bible verse in support of the death penalty constitute scriptural endorsement? No, it's not that simple. First of all, what is the Old Testament? It's the Christian reading of the Hebrew Bible understood as the inspired telling of Israel's story of coming to know the living God—a story that does not reach its conclusion until the coming of Israel's Messiah. Christians start their reading of the Bible with Christ, not the Torah. The entire Bible must be interpreted in the light of Christ, not apart from it. Christians can't camp out at some point in the Old Testament and pretend this is the final revelation of God's nature and will.

The writer of the epistle to the Hebrews, who appears to have been a Jewish priest, says,

> Long ago God spoke to our ancestors in many and various ways by the prophets, but in these last days he has spoken to us by a Son, whom he appointed heir of all things, through whom he also created the worlds. He is the reflection of God's glory and the exact imprint of God's very being. (Heb 1:1-3)

The Old Testament must be interpreted in the light of Christ, not used as case law to refute Christ. To cite the Old Testament as biblical evidence in support of the death penalty is to play the theologically impoverished game of proof texting.

What *can't* we "prove" through biblical proof texting? Wars of conquest, the practice of genocide, the institution of slavery, women held as property all have biblical proof texts, but no one in their right mind today believes that any of these things are morally justifiable, much less the will of God. (And lest I appear ill-disposed toward Judaism, let me emphasize that the ancient Hebrews as God's chosen people were leading the way toward justice in a Bronze Age world where all these types of injustices were normative.)

The question isn't whether we can find it in the Bible, but whether we can find it in Christ. Wars of conquest, ethnic cleansing, the institution of slavery, and women held as property can all be cited as biblical, but they are certainly not what we find in Christ. Christians who use the Torah for support of the death penalty generally want to apply it to murders and rapists. But why stop there? If biblical proof texting is to be our guide, why not call for the death penalty for rebellious teenagers? "If someone has a stubborn and rebellious son . . . all the men of the town shall stone him to death" (Deut 21:18, 21). And here is a point of enormous significance for Christians who want to cite the Old Testament in support of the death penalty: Jewish support for the actual practice of the death penalty as set forth in their own Bible was abandoned ages ago!

Historically, the Jews have never been comfortable with the death penalty. The rabbis did not like killing people. They made it all but impossible to jump through the strict legal requirements needed to warrant an execution. The Talmud, which collects rabbinic wisdom and guidance about Scripture, says of the process required for execution, "They rendered the execution of the death sentence all but impossible." The Mishnah, another source of rabbinic reflection, considers a court that passed the death penalty only once in seven years to be overly zealous. Other rabbis said one execution in seventy years is too many.[1]

We must not pretend that a biblical proof text amounts to the apex of biblical revelation. Sure, we can find Torah texts that condone the death penalty for certain crimes, but there are other texts as well, such as Yahweh's declaration to the prophet Ezekiel, "Have I any pleasure in the death of the wicked, says the Lord God, and not rather that they should turn away from their ways and live?" (Ezek 18:23).

Of course for Christians the final interpretation of the Old Testament belongs to Christ. When the scribes and Pharisees brought an adulterous woman to Jesus and said, "In the law Moses commanded us to stone such women. Now what do you say?" (Jn 8:5), we all know that the story ends with Jesus defending the woman and saying, "Neither do I condemn you. Go your way, and from now on do not sin again" (Jn 8:11). In other words, when Jesus was presented with a biblically supported death penalty case, he refused to support it. Any attempt to be more biblical than Jesus is a sure path to bad theology!

In 2014, Southern Baptist theologian and ethicist Albert Mohler wrote an opinion piece for CNN on "Why Christians should support the death penalty."[2] But in his twelve-hundred-word essay, Mohler never once cites or even mentions Jesus! That's a rather glaring omission for a Christian theologian. We cannot create Christian ethics while ignoring Christ! Contemporary Christian support of the death penalty (a phenomenon that is uniquely American) is awkwardly out of step with Jesus Christ, the early church, and the church fathers. As Shane Claiborne observes, "In the end, Christians in favor of the death penalty not only have the nagging problem of Jesus, but as we have seen, they are sharply at odds with the first three hundred years of Christianity."[3]

It's common for American evangelicals to cite Paul's warning in Romans 13 about the imperial state not bearing the sword in vain as a proof text for Christian support for the death penalty. But in his admonition against Christians joining the anti-Roman revolutionary movements that were fomenting at the time, leading to the First Jewish War in AD 66, Paul is simply stating that which is the case: If you participate in violent revolution against the imperial state, don't be surprised if you get put to death by the imperial sword. Paul is merely observing that pagan governments do, in fact, practice the death penalty. But Paul's command to Roman *Christians* is quite different: "Do not be overcome by evil, but overcome evil with good" (Rom 12:21).

To argue that evil is overcome by good through the death penalty, one would have to argue that death is good. And that is to do theology in a theater of the absurd. Evil was overcome at the cross, not by an imperial execution, but by the triumph of divine love. We are not saved by capital punishment; we are saved by the forgiving grace and resurrecting power of the one who was unjustly executed.

AMERICAN EXCEPTIONALISM

The ethics of capital punishment as interpreted in the light of the cross is a particularly pressing concern for American Christians. The United States is an outlier among democratic nations when it comes to the death penalty. For all practical purposes, the death penalty is only practiced by Islamic states, totalitarian states, and the United States. And widespread Christian support for the death penalty is uniquely American. Global evangelicals do not share the American evangelical enthusiasm for the death penalty. The myth of redemptive violence has such a hold on the American religious imagination that it even distorts how the cross is viewed. Millions of American Christians view the cross as a death penalty that God inflicted upon Jesus to satisfy justice rather than what it actually was: an unjust death penalty inflicted by a sinful world upon God in Christ. Stephen, the first Christian martyr, described the death of Jesus as a murder when he told the Sanhedrin, "You have become his betrayers and murderers" (Acts 7:52). Jesus was not killed by his Father; he was murdered by the religious establishment. And justice is never achieved by murder!

Bryan Stevenson, a Christian law professor, director of the Equal Justice Initiative, and author of the *New York Times* #1 bestseller *Just Mercy*, asks this disturbing question: "If it's not right to torture someone for torture, abuse someone for abuse, rape someone for rape, then how can we think we can kill someone for killing?"[4] And then there's the deeply troubling issue of executing innocent people— something Christians should instinctively connect with the cross of Christ. Since 1973, 187 persons on death row have been released from prison after it was discovered they were *innocent of the crime for which they were sentenced to death!*[5] One hundred and five of these exonerations have occurred since 2000. In other words, every other month or so we discover that a person sentenced to death is innocent!

Are we to assume that all wrongful convictions in capital crimes are discovered? Of course not. In the pursuit of justice how many executions of innocent people are acceptable? The answer is none! In the name of the innocent one condemned to the cross by Pontius Pilate, Christians must condemn capital punishment as sheer barbarism. In the twenty-first century we've tried to sanitize modern executions by employing the method of lethal injection, but have we failed to notice how closely a lethal injection table resembles a cross?

Central to the problem of American Christian support for the death penalty is the mistake of confusing justice with punishment. Justice is *not* punishment. Punishment *may* be part of a restorative process, but punishment for the sake of punishment is never justice— it is merely vengeance. Vengeance for the sake of vengeance is not found in the heart of God. Punishment as mere retribution does *not* satisfy justice. Justice is the work of rectification, setting to right that which is wrong. But retribution is not rectification. To murder a murderer does not set anything right, it merely increases murder. The justice of God can never be satisfied by an execution. This is a truth that needs to be thoroughly incorporated into our theology.

CAPITAL PUNISHMENT AND THE EARLY CHURCH

Purely punitive justice was not part of the Christian concept of criminal justice during the era of the early church. They only embraced that which could bring restoration to the victim and contribute to the eventual restoration of the criminal as justice. This is evidenced in the consistent patristic aversion to capital punishment.

In the year 412, two presbyters in the diocese of Hippo were attacked; one was killed and the other injured. Fearing that the attackers would be sentenced to execution or maiming for their crimes, Saint Augustine, the bishop of Hippo, wrote a letter to Judge Marcellinus in which he says,

> We do not wish the suffering of the servants of God avenged by the infliction of precisely similar injuries in way of retaliation. Not, of course, that we object to the removal from these wicked men of the liberty to perpetuate further crimes; but our desire is rather that justice be satisfied without the taking of their lives or the maiming of their bodies in any part. . . . Be not provoked by the atrocity of their sinful deeds to gratify the passion of revenge, but rather be moved by the wounds which these deeds have inflicted on their own souls to exercise a desire to heal them.[6]

For Augustine, the ideal of justice could only be satisfied when motivated by a desire to heal the souls of those who had committed murder. Augustine understood that a purely punitive punishment could not satisfy justice because it could not heal or restore. He stressed that a carnal desire for vengeance was abhorrent to Christian ethics because it was antithetical to the ways of the crucified Christ. His opposition to maiming or executing criminals was neither extreme nor unique; it was simply the common view of the early church.

Unfortunately, as the church became increasingly incorporated into the imperial state, it eventually lost its opposition to capital punishment as a Christ-informed ethic, and by the Middle Ages the church itself was actively involved in issuing death sentences. During the Reformation, John Calvin supported the execution of the heretical Spanish theologian Michael Servetus in Geneva in 1553, justifying his endorsement of the death sentence with a particularly egregious line of reasoning.

> There is no question here of man's authority; it is God who speaks and clear it is what law he will have kept in the Church, even to the end of the world. Wherefore does he demand of us a so extreme severity, if not to show us that due honor is not paid him, so long as we set not his service above every human consideration, so that we spare not kin nor blood of any, and forget all humanity when the matter is to combat for His glory.[7]

In this sad incident from the life of John Calvin we see how a dreadful theology led a good man astray. Just as Calvin attributed the crucifixion of Jesus to the actions of God, he also projects upon God his own desire to have Michael Servetus burned at the stake. In denying the Trinity, the theology of Servetus was indeed heretical, but that does not justify an argument that in the name of God we must "forget all humanity" in order to "combat for His glory."

The moment we forget that all humans, including heretics, bear the image of God, we have opened the door for all kinds of atrocities. As the primary architect of the modern penal atonement theory, Calvin imagined God as a wrathful deity who required appeasement by torture and execution. Thus it is little wonder that Calvin could conclude that the burning of heretics in the name of God was the "law he will have kept in the Church." Calvin's theology of the violent appeasement of a vengeful God blinded him to the real law that God would have kept in the church. James the brother of Jesus sets it forth like this: "If you really fulfill the royal law according to the scripture, 'You shall love your neighbor as yourself,' you do well" (Jas 2:8). Calvin's penal theology that posited God as punishing his Son on the cross is directly related to Calvin's absurd notion that God could be honored by the city of Geneva by burning at the stake a fellow human being. Bad theology has real-life consequences.

Moving Forward by Reaching Back

The church can turn away from bad theology and make progress by returning to its roots. This was the philosophy that inspired the *Ressourcement* movement in Catholic theology in the twentieth century. Theologians like Henri de Lubac, Yves Congar, Jean Daniélou, Hans Urs von Balthasar, and Joseph Ratzinger led the way out of moribund medieval theology toward a future-looking theology by returning to the sources of the early church. Rather than retaining the imperial theology that had ingratiated itself with the state by supplying theological support for imperial violence like war and capital punishment, the theological sources that existed prior to imperial entanglement were privileged. The result has been a Catholic Church of the twenty-first century that is increasingly bold in its prophetic opposition to war and the death penalty.

On October 3, 2020, Pope Francis issued an encyclical titled "Fratelli Tutti" ("All Brothers"). An entire section of the encyclical is dedicated to clarifying that the Catholic Church is opposed to the death penalty in all cases. The section begins like this:

> There is yet another way to eliminate others, one aimed not at countries but at individuals. It is the death penalty. Saint John Paul II stated clearly and firmly that the death penalty is inadequate from a moral standpoint and no longer necessary from that of penal justice. There can be no stepping back from this position. Today we state clearly that "the death penalty is inadmissible" and the Church is firmly committed to calling for its abolition worldwide.[8]

It's heartening to hear the ecclesial leader of more than a billion Christians returning to the pro-life position of the early church regarding the death penalty. Christ upon the cross is the eternal moment when war, capital punishment, and all other forms of state-sponsored killing are forever condemned.

In a civil society, violent criminals must be incarcerated, but they must not be tortured and executed. Nearly all nations that have been significantly influenced by Christianity understand this. Yet, in this regard, America remains a barbarous outlier. I pray that new and creative preaching on the cross can generate significant change in the American religious consciousness.

15

THE SWORD-PIERCED SOUL OF MARY

At the Cross her station keeping,
Stood the mournful Mother weeping,
Close to Jesus to the last:
Through her heart, his sorrow sharing,
All his bitter anguish bearing,
now at length the sword has pass'd.

"STABAT MATER," THIRTEENTH-CENTURY HYMN

WHEN I BEGAN WRITING THIS BOOK, I had not intended to include a chapter on Mary, the mother of Jesus. But then I had a dream in which I wrote a chapter on the significance of Mary's sorrow as she stood near the cross of her son on Good Friday. Apparently, my subconscious, with perhaps a nudge from the Holy Spirit, knew I needed to explore the sword-pierced soul of Mary. I'm glad I dreamed of writing this chapter.

It should be noted I'm a Protestant by default. I'm not really protesting anything, but because I'm neither Orthodox nor Catholic, I land somewhere in the vast and fragmented world of Protestantism.

For the most part, Protestants have been wary of Mary, and some of the wariness is understandable. I've visited many a baroque-era Catholic church in Portugal where Jesus clearly comes in a distant second among the statuary and religious art when compared to the devotion paid to the Virgin. But as I said, I'm not really protesting anything. I understand that the various expressions of Christian religion develop along different trajectories, and I'm fine with that.

Today I'm a deeply ecumenical Christian and I feel quite at home worshiping with Orthodox and Catholic believers. I've recited the Hail Mary with monks in a Benedictine monastery as we prayed our way through the fourteen Stations of the Cross during Lent. And though I think the Catholic doctrine of the Immaculate Conception of Mary (a doctrine only formally adopted in the nineteenth century and not to be confused with the Virgin Birth of Christ) is an unnecessary theological move, I have no interest in tempering Catholic veneration of Mary. My concern is that the virtual absence of Mary in Protestant thought is just as problematic as an excessive emphasis on Mary is in certain forms of Catholicism.

THE THEOTOKOS

In Christian theology Mary bears the title of Theotokos, the mother of God (or literally God-bearer). Mary is not, of course, the matrix of the Trinity, but as God becomes human in Christ, Mary becomes the mother of God. To be human is to have a mother, and through the incarnation the Virgin Mary truly became the one who gave birth to God. "Mother of God" (rather than merely "Mother of Christ") as the theologically correct title for Mary was established at the Council of Ephesus in 431. Acknowledging Mary as such is a theological necessity for a high Christology, as Cyril of Alexandria understood. A hesitancy to affirm Mary as the Mother of God fails to take seriously the Nicene confession that Jesus Christ is "true God from true God."

From meditation on the christological mystery of the Theotokos came the sixth-century Byzantine Akathist hymn still sung in Orthodox churches today. One of its twenty-four verses says this:

> You were made more spacious than the heavens,
> O Most Pure Mother,
> for God cannot be contained by the whole universe,
> and yet He chose to be contained in your womb for the sake
>   of our salvation.[1]

I had visited Orthodox churches in Greece, Russia, and the Middle East long before I ever visited an Orthodox church in the United States. It was on my first visit to an American Orthodox church that I read in English the words "more spacious than the heavens" on the Theotokos icon on the apse above the altar. It's how I became aware of the Akathist hymn and its theology of the Theotokos. These words poetically convey the theological mystery that the Creator who contains the cosmos became the conceived who was contained in the womb of Mary.

Let me state this mystery more emphatically. The Creator of a universe that contains at least a hundred billion galaxies with two-hundred-billion-trillion stars became a fetus in a uterus! In a theo-poetic sense the womb of Mary was indeed "more spacious than the heavens." The more we meditate on this mystery the more profound it becomes, and this mystery draws our attention not only to the eternal Logos who became flesh, but to the virgin who gave flesh to the Logos.

Mary is both a holy mystery and an enduring archetype. All of us should say with Mary, "Here am I, the servant of the Lord; let it be with me according to your word" (Lk 1:38). All of us should in some way seek to enflesh the word of God in our lives. But Mary is also utterly unique. The virgin of Nazareth is the one through whom the eternal Logos became human. All women can be called the handmaiden of the Lord, but only one woman can be called the mother of God. Thus the angel Gabriel's salutation, "Rejoice, highly favored one, the Lord is with you; blessed are you among women!" (Lk 1:28 NKJV). Mary is a holy mystery that we should thoroughly explore theologically and devotionally, Protestant hesitancies notwithstanding.

The story of Mary begins with the angelic annunciation in Nazareth followed by her three-month stay in the hill country of Judea with her cousin Elizabeth, who was six months pregnant with John the Baptist, and Mary's prophetic Magnificat anticipating the arrival of a revolutionary kingdom through the two boys soon to be born. The story continues with Mary and Joseph's long journey to Bethlehem, the drama of finding no room in the inn, and Jesus' birth among the livestock where he is wrapped in swaddling clothes and laid in a manger.

Forty days later, Mary and Joseph took Jesus to the temple to perform the rites of dedication. While there they encountered Simeon, a righteous and devout old man to whom it had been revealed that he would not see death until he had first seen the Messiah. Prompted by the Spirit, Simeon took the baby Jesus in his arms and prayed,

> Master, now you are dismissing your servant in peace,
>> according to your word;
> for my eyes have seen your salvation,
>> which you have prepared in the presence of all peoples,
> a light for revelation to the gentiles
>> and for glory to your people Israel. (Lk 2:29-32)

After his prayer of thanksgiving, Simeon began to prophesy how the child was destined for the falling and rising of many in Israel. Last, he turned to Mary and spoke an ominous word: "And a sword will pierce your own soul, too" (Lk 2:35).

One wonders what Mary thought of Simeon's dark portent. Yet isn't this prophecy true for all of us? No one makes it through life unscathed. Behind every beautiful thing there's been some kind of pain. The sword of sorrow eventually pierces every heart. Again we see how Mary is both unique in her vocation and yet an archetype for all of us.

OUR LADY OF SORROWS

During my travels in Spain, I've seen many statues of Our Lady of Sorrows in Catholic churches. The statue depicts a swooning Mary with seven swords piercing her chest. Typically this is not a carved stone statue, but a mannequin bedecked with real clothes, real hair, and real swords. I'll admit that my artistic (and perhaps northern Protestant) tastes find this sort of thing too macabre and maudlin. It feels a bit too much like something from a Halloween haunted house. I decidedly prefer the more subdued dignity of an Orthodox icon. One can discern Mary's sorrow in the twelfth century *Virgin of Vladimir* icon without the garishness of the seven swords.

Nevertheless there is a message to be understood in the statue pierced with seven swords. The first time I saw Our Lady of Sorrows in a Spanish church, I knew it represented Simeon's prophecy, but why *seven* swords? I later learned they represent the Seven Sorrows of Mary in Catholic tradition: Simeon's prophecy, the flight to Egypt, the loss of the child Jesus in Jerusalem, meeting her son on the Via Dolorosa from medieval legend, the crucifixion, Jesus taken down from the cross, and his burial in the tomb of Joseph of Arimathea. Surely these were sorrows that would pierce a mother's heart.

And I could add at least one more. After Jesus left his home in Nazareth to be baptized in Judea and returned to Galilee to begin his ministry, he did not come back to Nazareth but instead relocated to Capernaum. As Jesus' popularity grew in Galilee, news soon reached Nazareth. Mark is unsparing in reporting the reaction of Jesus' family to what was happening. "When his family heard about this, they went to take charge of him, for they said, 'He is out of his mind'" (Mk 3:21 NIV).

Mark continues, unsparing in his reporting.

Then his mother and his brothers came, and standing outside they sent to him and called him. . . . And they said to him, "Your mother and your brothers are outside asking for you." And he replied, "Who are my mother and my brothers?" And looking at those who sat around him, he said, "Here are my mother and my brothers! Whoever does the will of God is my brother and sister and mother." (Mk 3:31-35)

There is much more to say about this episode than will be said here. Of one thing we can be certain: words like this would be a dagger to the heart of any mother.

MARY AT GOLGOTHA

Whatever initial misgivings Mary had about her son's prophetic vocation, she was among the women who followed him to Jerusalem for the final time, and she was with him at the end. Mary was at Golgotha. Mary saw her son crucified. She witnessed the death of her firstborn, the cruelest sword of all. It's John the Evangelist who gives us this poignant scene.

Standing near the cross of Jesus were his mother, and his mother's sister, Mary the wife of Clopas, and Mary Magdalene. When Jesus saw his mother and the disciple whom he loved standing beside her, he said to his mother, "Woman, here is your son." Then he said to the disciple, "Here is your mother." And from that hour the disciple took her into his own home. (Jn 19:25-27)

From his cross Jesus sees a group of women and the beloved disciple. The Evangelist focuses on Jesus entrusting his mother to the beloved disciple, but Christian imagination has focused on the mother's sorrow. And how can it not? For a parent to lose a child is the most painful wound of all. And for a mother to witness her son's crucifixion is an inconceivable agony.

Surely this is the sword of which Simeon spoke. The angel had told the young virgin she was highly favored, and the aged seer had told her a sword would pierce her soul. Both prophecies turned out to be true. Only one woman could be the favored Theotokos, but the honor came with a sword of sorrow that would pierce her soul. To be chosen and elect by God for a unique vocation is no guarantee of ease and happiness. It usually comes with a call to participate in redemptive suffering. Just ask Abraham or Jeremiah or Peter or Paul or Mary.

It's not from the biblical text that we find depictions of Mary's sorrow at the cross, but from Christian art, especially sculptures, paintings, and hymns. Art draws our attention to what we may have overlooked. The thirteenth-century hymn "Stabat Mater" ("Sorrowful Mother"), Michelangelo's *Pietà*, and countless paintings and icons of Mary mourning at the cross have invited Christians to contemplate the depths of sorrow the mother of God endured as she grieved the death of God who was simultaneously her son. And for those enduring their own sorrows, these images, hymns, and meditations on the sorrowful mother of God have not compounded sorrow but have been a source of solace. Mary is understood as one who mourns with us.

MOURNING WITH MARY

One of the follies characterizing much of Western modernity is the assumption that we moderns are somehow exempt from the experience of sorrow and the bitter work of grief. It is tacitly implied that if we have enough security, technology, and money we should be able to get through life without being pierced by sorrow. This philosophy is particularly prominent in a military-economic superpower. Inconsolable grief is a plight that befalls those unfortunate souls not blessed to live as a citizen of the greatest nation on earth, or so the propaganda would lead us to believe.

The book of Revelation lampoons this kind of imperial hubris. The biblical opposite of the Virgin Mary is the whore of Babylon. John the Revelator personifies the Roman Empire as a drunken harlot imperiously boasting, "I sit enthroned as queen. I am not a widow; I will never mourn" (Rev 18:7 NIV). Mourning is considered beneath the dignity of the empire. But the mother of God mourns. The mother of God is pierced with a sword of sorrow. The mother of God does not deny grief as she beholds her son hanging upon a cross.

The attempt to avoid the possibility of pain and deny the work of grief is an attempt to be something other than human. In the mystery of the incarnation, God assumes mortality through Mary, and when the God-Man succumbs to mortality on the cross, Mary must mourn over the loss of her child. That she would mourn as one grieving her firstborn became inevitable the moment she said, "Let it be with me according to your word" (Lk 1:38). Her mourning confers dignity upon all who mourn.

We moderns need to learn how to mourn like Mary. I'm troubled by the rise of the modern neurosis of death denial and grief avoidance. I increasingly hear of people buried or cremated without any kind of funeral service. It's as though the living are not to be troubled by the dead, even if they are family members. To die ungrieved was a horrid curse in ages past, but now it's become aspirational. It's increasingly common to hear funeral attendance dismissed with the paltry excuse, "I don't do funerals," as if grief can be circumvented simply by refusing to attend a funeral.

This is something entirely novel in human history. It's also unhealthy. A celebration of life involves sorrow at the loss of that life, even with the hope of resurrection. Paul wrote about such hope in his first letter to the Thessalonians saying, "And now, dear brothers and sisters, we want you to know what will happen to the believers who have died so you will not grieve like people who have no hope" (1 Thess 4:13 NLT). Paul's admonition was not that we should deny grief, but that we should grieve as those who hold to the hope of resurrection. The notion that people should deny grief altogether would never have occurred to Paul. Grieving is a work that must be done, and received wisdom knows that the work of grief is best done in the company of others. The medieval paintings of the grieving women at the cross of Christ contain far more wisdom than the modern denial of grief. From Mary we learn that sorrow is unavoidable, and that mourning is a work that is both necessary and holy.

The final time Mary is mentioned in the Bible is when she is named among those gathered in the upper room awaiting the outpouring of the Holy Spirit on the day of Pentecost. "All these were constantly devoting themselves to prayer, together with certain women, including Mary the mother of Jesus" (Acts 1:14). Mary had known the sorrow of her son's death and she shared in the joy of his resurrection. Did Jesus personally appear to his mother following his resurrection? The Scriptures don't tell us, so we are left to wonder, though it's hard to imagine that the risen Jesus did not appear to his mother. What we can be sure of is that the one who brought Jesus into the world through birth was received by her Son at the time of her death.

Dormition Abbey is a Benedictine monastery on Mount Zion marking the traditional site of Mary's death, *dormition* being the Latin word for "sleep." Though Christians have venerated this site since the early fifth century, the current basilica was dedicated in 1910. The crypt in the basilica—the traditional site of Mary's death, or as Catholic's would say, her assumption—contains a fresco that is one of my favorite images in Christian art. It depicts Mary lying in repose upon her deathbed surrounded by the apostles. Standing above Mary, Christ gazes down at his mother, holding in his arms a small child wrapped in swaddling clothes. As you look closely at the fresco you realize that the face of Mary in repose is the face of the swaddled child held in the arms of Jesus. An inscription in Greek at the top of the fresco reads "The Dormition of the Theotokos."

What we see in this fresco is a reversal of *Madonna and Child*. As Mary held her son wrapped in swaddling clothes, Jesus now holds his mother wrapped in grave clothes. As Mary gave Jesus mortal life,

Jesus now gives Mary eternal life. Through the Theotokos, the Logos gained mortality that through death he might conquer death and save mortal humanity. The Theotokos serves the ultimate telos of humanity: theosis. As Saint Athanasius said in his famous treatise on the incarnation, "God became man that man might become God."[2] Peter's second epistle describes theosis as becoming "participants of the divine nature" (2 Pet 1:4). We can become participants in the divine nature, the very essence of salvation, only because the divine became a participant in human nature. And this participation came about through the Theotokos.

As Mary the mother of God was present at the cross, so she is present throughout the entire mystery of incarnation.

Hail Mary, full of grace,
the Lord is with thee.
Blessed art thou among women,
and blessed is the fruit of thy womb, Jesus.
Holy Mary, Mother of God,
pray for us sinners,
now and at the hour of our death. Amen.

16

THREE TREES
ON THE LOW SKY

Then at dawn we came to a temperate valley,
Wet, below the snow line, smelling of vegetation,
With a running stream and a water-mill beating the darkness,
And three trees on the low sky.

T. S. ELIOT, "JOURNEY OF THE MAGI"

WHEN WE THINK OF CRUCIFIXION we instinctively, and for obvious reasons, think of the crucifixion of Jesus Christ. When we speak of the crucified one, we know of whom we speak. In the iconography and religious art of the crucifixion, Christ is often portrayed as a lone victim. And if we're not historically informed on the subject, we may imagine crucifixion as something that was rare and exotic. But this was not the case. The Roman Empire carried out hundreds of thousands of crucifixions.

In the year 4 BC the Roman general Varus crucified two thousand Jewish rebels at Sepphoris—a small Galilean city four miles from Nazareth. During the siege of Jerusalem in AD 70 the Roman legions crucified so many people that they ran out of trees! If you lived in Roman-occupied Judea in the first century you would likely have seen crucifixions. Because their primary purpose was to psychologically intimidate an occupied people into subservience, the Romans crucified their victims in public places and along major thoroughfares. Crucifixions were not rare and exotic; they were disturbingly common.

One of the scandals of Good Friday is that Jesus was not even afforded the smallest dignity of being a lone spectacle—he was but one of three crucifixions that day. Two criminals were led away to be put to death with him. When they came to the place that is called The Skull, they crucified Jesus there with the criminals, one on his right and one on his left (Lk 23:32-33).

Jesus Barabbas

Three criminals were supposed to be crucified at The Skull on Good Friday, but Jesus was nailed to a cross that had been intended for someone else. Matthew gives us the full name of this criminal who was slated for crucifixion and received a last-minute pardon. "At that time they had a notorious prisoner called Jesus Barabbas" (Mt 27:16). This Jesus Barabbas (meaning "Jesus Son of the Father") was a rebel leader who had committed murder during an insurrection. He wasn't a common killer, but a revolutionary guerrilla fighter and a hero to many in Jerusalem.

This explains why the crowd at Pilate's headquarters could easily be persuaded to ask for his release.

> Pilate said to them, "Whom do you want me to release for you, Jesus Barabbas or Jesus who is called the Messiah?" . . . Now the chief priests and the elders persuaded the crowds to ask for Barabbas and to have Jesus killed. The governor again said to them, "Which of the two do you want me to release for you?" And they said, "Barabbas." (Mt 27:17, 20-21)

In the eyes of the Romans, Barabbas was a terrorist, but in the eyes of many Jews he was a freedom fighter. Think of Barabbas as a first-century Jewish William Wallace or Che Guevara and you get the idea.

As a rebel leader willing to kill Roman soldiers and their Jewish collaborators for the sake of political liberation, Jesus "Son of the Father" was a messianic alternative to Jesus of Nazareth. These two men named Yeshua (salvation) are two visions of salvation. While Jesus Barabbas was willing to take up lethal arms in violent revolution, Jesus of Nazareth stretched out his arms of love upon the hard wood of the cross. The Barabbas way of salvation comes by killing; the Jesus way of salvation comes by dying. Jesus died for our sins— and in the most literal way possible, he died for Barabbas. Following the resurrection, Peter confronted those who had asked for the release of Barabbas by saying, "You rejected the holy and righteous one and asked to have a murderer given to you, and you killed the author of life, whom God raised from the dead" (Acts 3:14-15). Yes, Barabbas was quite literally saved by Jesus taking his place on the cross.

This act of being counted as a criminal and bearing the sin of others is anticipated at the end of Isaiah's Suffering Servant song.

> He poured out himself to death,
>   and was numbered with the transgressors,
> yet he bore the sin of many
>   and made intercession for the transgressors. (Is 53:12)

At Golgotha, we see not one, but three crosses. Jesus was crucified, not as a lone martyr, but as Emmanuel among the sufferers. Through the incarnation God joined humanity in its common lot of suffering. As Jesus hung crucified between two fellow sufferers, he descended into the depths of Isaiah's prophecy that the servant of the Lord would be "a man of suffering, and familiar with pain" (Is 53:3 NIV). For God to become human is for God to experience suffering. To be human is to suffer.

The inevitability of suffering is a truth recognized in all religions. There is no escaping it. But not all suffering is the same. Suffering for an honorable purpose is more bearable and can even be ennobling. But so much of the suffering that comes upon us is pointless. Most of it comes not from a noble cause but from the cruel vagaries of life. If suffering is inevitable and pointless, it is an inevitable pointlessness endured by God in Christ. Yet once God is involved with something, it can no longer be pointless. There is no nihilism in God. The incarnation is purposeful, never pointless. Christ takes upon himself the pointless suffering of the world for the purpose of redeeming it all through his co-suffering love. "By his wounds you have been healed" (1 Pet 2:24).

Suffering is inevitable, but it does not have the last word. Paul can say, "I consider that the sufferings of this present time are not worth comparing with the glory about to be revealed to us" (Rom 8:18). The only credible Christian theodicy is that in Christ God fully participates in human suffering, and that suffering is not the end of the story. "Creation itself will be set free from its enslavement to decay and will obtain the freedom of the glory of the children of God" (Rom 8:21). And even in our present age of suffering, no one suffers alone. Christ is present to every sufferer as the crucified one. Every crucifix speaks to those who are suffering, "You are not alone. I am with you in your suffering." This is part of what we see in the trio of crosses upon Calvary's hill.

THE GREAT DIVIDE

It's true that Jesus was numbered among the transgressors and shared a solidarity with their agony, an act of co-suffering love that is redemptive. But it is also true that Jesus is the dividing point. Jesus is not just with the two criminals, he is *between* them—one on his right, one on his left. The cross of Christ is the great judgment that divides humanity.

All four Gospels report that Jesus was crucified between two criminals, but Luke most clearly presents Jesus as the point of separation between the two. Though it is currently in vogue to resist any duality in Christian theology, Jesus' parables are full of radical dichotomies: the sheep and the goats, the wise and foolish virgins, the wise and foolish builders, the good and bad fish, the obedient and disobedient sons, the Pharisee and the tax collector. And on Good Friday we discover a dichotomy portrayed in the two criminals crucified with Jesus. These two men had much in common—both were convicted brigands, presumably partners in crime, who suffered the same fate. But by the end of the day they were divided by Jesus in a radical way. As Jesus said in his final parable before his passion, the Son of Man upon his glorious throne separates the sheep and the goats. The glorious throne of the Son of Man is his cross.

Three were crucified that day, but it was the famous preacher and miracle worker from Galilee who drew the gawking crowd to Golgotha. They jeered at Jesus for claiming that he would destroy and rebuild the temple in three days. The priests who had orchestrated Jesus' arrest and condemnation were there to gloat. They "scoffed at him, saying, 'He saved others; let him save himself if he is the Messiah of God, his chosen one!'" (Lk 23:35). As they gambled for his clothes, the Roman soldiers mocked Jesus by sarcastically calling him the King of the Jews.

The contagion that causes a crowd to unify around a vilified scapegoat was spreading. Eventually even one of the men being crucified was caught up in the contagion and began "deriding him and saying, 'Are you not the Messiah? Save yourself and us!'" (Lk 23:39). This reveals just how powerful the satanic lure of scapegoating can be. Here we see a crucified man finding a perverse consolation in joining the crowd as they accuse another man who is also being crucified! As he is dying, he finds sadistic solace in joining the accusation of the scapegoat.

Blame is a powerful narcotic. Yet somehow the other criminal did not join the crowd or his fellow brigand in accusing Jesus.

> But the other rebuked him, saying, "Do you not fear God, since you are under the same sentence of condemnation? And we indeed have been condemned justly, for we are getting what we deserve for our deeds, but this man has done nothing wrong."

Then he said, "Jesus, remember me when you come in your kingdom." (Lk 23:40-42)

One of the recurring themes in the Gospels is how all the "wrong" people demonstrate the most surprising faith in Jesus. Roman centurions, tax collectors, Gentile women, and even prostitutes are commended by Jesus for the greatness of their faith. But in my mind, the dying thief outdoes them all. He sees in Jesus what the crowd does not see—he sees his innocence. And he dares to proclaim it. When the crowd has selected its scapegoat and begins to pile on the accusations, it takes profound insight and enormous courage to say, "This man has done nothing wrong."

But more than his innocence, he saw Jesus' true identity. Where the crowd sees an impostor getting his due comeuppance, the dying thief sees a king coming into his kingdom. Not even the faithful women who remained at the cross dared to believe that Jesus was entering into his kingdom . . . but the dying thief does! Jesus has been mockingly derided by the chief priests, the Roman soldiers, and the jeering crowd. Pilate's sarcastic inscription written in three languages and affixed to his cross read, "Jesus of Nazareth, the King of the Jews" (Jn 19:19). But the dying thief actually *believes* it!

As the thief heard Jesus derided as the Christ, faith arose in his heart that this man *really was* the Christ! Not only that, he also apparently knew the prophecy found at the conclusion of the book of Daniel proclaiming a resurrection at the end of the age. The dying thief believed that Jesus was the messianic king who would reign in the age to come. So he prayed to the king, "Jesus, remember me when you come into your kingdom."

The dying thief's prayer to be remembered by Israel's true king is deliberately reminiscent of David's prayer in Psalm 25:7, "Do not remember the sins of my youth or my transgressions; according to your steadfast love *remember me*, for the sake of your goodness, O Lord!" (emphasis added). The dying thief prays to Jesus in the same way that David prayed to God. The thief admits that his youth has been full of sin, but he asks Jesus to remember not his transgressions, but to remember *him*. The dying thief seems to be praying something like this: "Jesus, I believe you are the King, the Christ, the Messiah. And I have sinned. But I'm more than my sins. For the sake of your goodness and steadfast love remember me for who I really am and save me." It's hard to imagine a better sinner's prayer than that.

How did Jesus respond to the dying sinner's plea to be remembered in mercy? With these famous words: "Truly I tell you, today you will be with me in paradise" (Lk 23:43). Before the sun would set that day this repentant sinner would die, but he would not be lost. He would be safe with Jesus in Paradise awaiting resurrection. He would be remembered by his Savior. To be remembered by Jesus is salvation.

To die is to eventually be forgotten, but to be remembered by God is to be redeemed from the finality of death. Once we die, we are fated to eventually be forgotten by those in the land of the living. Once I'm dead and gone I'm sure my children and grandchildren will remember me, but as the generations roll by, I'll eventually be forgotten. The psalmist calls the grave "the land of forgetfulness" (Ps 88:12). But Jesus will remember me. This is the hope of resurrection.

What about the other thief? He also prays from his cross, but his prayer is cynical and mocking. He views Jesus not according to faith, but according to the crowd. One criminal sees in Jesus the possibility of a new kind of kingdom characterized by mercy, and he believes. The other criminal, though a victim himself, cannot resist participating with the crowd in blaming a victim. Good Friday with its three crosses presents the choice in a most dramatic way, but we are presented the same choice nearly every day. We can follow Jesus in the way of mercy—"Father, forgive them"—or we can follow the crowd in the way of accusation—"Crucify him!" But only one way leads to the paradise of union with Christ.

When we deal with our fear and anger and pain and shame by projecting blame on others, we achieve a union with the satanic spirit of accusation that produces a temporary catharsis, but also keeps us locked in our own self-imposed hell. In the parable of the prodigal son the story ends not with the return of the wayward son, but with his elder brother refusing to attend the homecoming party in the father's house. He stands outside the house bitterly accusing his brother. He is in the outer darkness. "In that place there will be weeping and gnashing of teeth" (Mt 8:12 ESV). The elder brother is in hell. But it is a self-imposed hell. As C.S. Lewis once suggested, "The doors of hell are locked on the *inside.*"[1]

The good news is that there is a way out of this self-imposed hell. If we can see in the crucified one the possibility of a new kingdom founded on forgiveness and follow our faith in that direction, we achieve a paradisiacal union with Christ . . . today! The believing thief died that day, but we, too, can die today. That's why Paul could say things like, "I have been crucified with Christ" (Gal 2:19), "I die every day" (1 Cor 15:31), and "You have died, and your life is hidden with Christ in God" (Col 3:3). As we look upon the crucified one, we can die to self-deceit and choose honesty; we can die to pride and choose humility; we can die to blame and choose mercy; we can die to disbelief and choose trust. As we do so, we enter a union with Christ experienced as a paradise of peace.

DON'T DESPAIR, DON'T PRESUME

Three trees on a low sky. The Son of Man upon his glorious throne separating the sheep and the goats. A drama of salvation and damnation. The brilliant Irish film *Calvary*, written and directed by John Michael McDonagh—a film that is both irreverent and deeply Christian—opens with these lines:[2]

> Do not despair; one of the thieves was saved.
> Do not presume; one of the thieves was damned.
> —Saint Augustine

Augustine's aphorism employed as the epigraph in *Calvary* speaks of despair and presumption. Don't despair; one was saved. Don't presume; one was damned. There's wisdom here. Despair is what led Judas to hang himself. Don't despair. Presumption is a poor substitute for faith. God is found by those who seek him, not by those who presume him. And yet there is something more to be said about despair and presumption as it applies to salvation and damnation.

I will never presume anyone is eternally damned. Not even Judas Iscariot. In *Unspoken Sermons* George MacDonald (whom C. S. Lewis regarded as his "master") writes this about the betrayer of Christ: "I think, when Judas fled from his hanged and fallen body, he fled to the tender help of Jesus, and found it—I say not how. . . . I believe that Jesus loved Judas even when he was kissing him with the traitor's kiss; and I believe that he was his Saviour still."[3] I share George MacDonald's hope that Judas was or will be saved, but like MacDonald I say not how.

Commenting on MacDonald's hope for the salvation of all, C. S. Lewis says,

> Reaction against early teachings might on this point have very easily driven him into a shallow liberalism. But it does not. He hopes, indeed, that all men will be saved; but that is because he hopes that all will repent. He knows (none better) that even omnipotence cannot save the unconverted. He never trifles with eternal impossibilities.[4]

Christ hanging upon the middle cross does indeed divide the saved and the damned. Amen. But can we not also hope that at the end of time the realm assigned to the damned might be empty? The unbelieving thief may have died deriding Christ, but that doesn't mean we've arrived at the end of his story. For in his wild pursuit of the lost, Christ will descend even into hell.

17

THE HARROWING
OF HELL

When you were nailed to the Cross, the might of the enemy was put to death. When you descended unto death, O Life Immortal, you slew Hades by the lightning of your divinity.

SAINT JOHN OF DAMASCUS

AT THIS POINT IT SHOULD BE EVIDENT that there is a myriad of meanings to the cross—not competing interpretations, but multiple achievements to be recognized. Though there are many accomplishments, the ultimate triumph of the cross is that it is the death by which death itself is destroyed. The death of God resulted in the death of death. The death of God dooms death itself to its own undoing. The crucifixion of Christ was not a defeat that was overturned by resurrection. Rather it was a victory revealed in resurrection.

In the light of Easter, we understand that Good Friday was never a defeat but always a conquest. It was the victory of a champion. It was the Son of David slaying the Goliath of death. It was, as a representative champion's victory is, a victory won on behalf of others. From Adam onward death reigned supreme over every son of Adam and daughter of Eve, imprisoning each in the shadowy world of

Sheol, incarcerating all in the grim netherworld of Hades. (The Jewish concept of Sheol and the Greek concept of Hades were more or less the same—an underworld imprisoning departed spirits.) But in the fullness of time the eternal Logos assumed mortality as our champion to take the field and do battle with death unto the death. The writer of Hebrews says, "Since, therefore, the children share flesh and blood, he himself likewise shared the same things, so that through death he might destroy the one who has the power of death, that is, the devil, and free those who all their lives were held in slavery by the fear of death" (Heb 2:14-15).

HELL AND DEATH IN EARLY CHRISTIAN HYMNS

For the early church fathers, especially those in the Greek-speaking East, the triumph of Christ over death was far and away the most common way they spoke about what had been accomplished by the cross. This was especially true in their hymns and liturgies. Atonement theology is shaped far more by the hymns we sing than by the sermons we hear. Sermons come and go, but the most popular hymns endure for centuries and influence our theological imagination more than we know.

The second-century Easter hymn still sung in Orthodox churches to this day reflects the earliest theology of the cross.

> Christ is risen from the dead,
> trampling down death by death,
> and upon those in the tombs bestowing life.[1]

The understanding that, through his death on the cross, Christ descended into Hades to defeat death is traditionally referred to as the "harrowing of hell," and it was the most common Easter theme for the early church. The harrowing of hell was regularly dramatized in sermons and hymns with brilliant and playful imagination.

An excellent example of early Christian imagination on Christ's harrowing of hell is seen in the second-century poem "On Easter" by

Saint Melito of Sardis. The poem was part of a Paschal sermon celebrating Christ's victory over Hades on behalf of humanity.

> The Lord, when he had clothed himself with man . . .
> arose from the dead and uttered this cry:
> " . . . I am the one who destroyed death
> and triumphed over the enemy
> and trod down Hades
> and bound the strong one.
> I carried off man to the heights of heaven;
> I am the one," says Christ.
> "Come then, all you families of men who are
> compounded with sins,
> and receive forgiveness of sins.
> For I am your forgiveness,
> I am the Pascha of salvation,
> I am the lamb slain for you;
> I am your ransom,
> I am your life,
> I am your light,
> I am your salvation,
> I am your resurrection,
> I am your king.
> I will raise you up by my right hand;
> I am leading you up to the heights of heaven;
> There I will show you the Father from ages past."[2]

Saint Melito has Christ say, "I am your ransom." This idea is drawn from the words of Jesus when he told his disciples, "The Son of Man came not to be served but to serve and to give his life a ransom for many" (Mk 10:45). The language of ransom was the most common metaphor used by the church fathers to interpret the cross. Modern theologians refer to this interpretation as the "ransom theory" of atonement, though the ancient Christians would not have called it a theory. For them it was simply the language they used to talk about Christ's triumph over death. But ransom language can be misleading for modern people if we follow Calvin's theory and imagine the death of Christ as a ransom *paid to God*. No!

Saint Basil the Great speaks of this when he says of Christ,

> He gave himself as *a ransom to death*, in which we were held captive, sold under sin. Descending through the Cross into hell that he might fill all things with himself, he loosed the pangs of death. He arose on the third day, having made for all flesh a path to the resurrection from the dead.[3]

The church fathers *always* spoke of the ransom being paid to death, or to the devil as a personification of death. Early Christian preachers were fond of speaking of the death of Christ as a kind of trick played on the devil. They spoke of the flesh of Christ as the bait on the hook of divinity. Because Jesus was mortal, he could be swallowed by death, but death could not digest divinity. The devil took the bait and swallowed the hook. Once divinity was swallowed by death, death itself became ill and doomed to die.

John Chrysostom, the most creative of the patristic preachers, was particularly fond of describing death as unable to digest Christ and vomiting him up as the whale had done with Jonah.

> As they who take food which they are unable to retain, on account of that vomit up also what was before lodged in them; so also it happened unto death. That Body, which he could not digest, he received: and therefore had to cast forth that which he had within him. Yea, he travailed in pain, whilst he held Him, and was straitened until he vomited him up.[4]

The death of Jesus upon the cross did not appease God but it did sicken death. This is the most common way the first Christians preached the cross. And they clearly enjoyed employing a mischievous imagination in taunting Satan, death, and hell. In his sermon "Homily on the Cemetery and the Cross," Chrysostom boldly asserts that "Christ by his death bound the chief of robbers and the jailer, that is, the devil and death, and transferred his treasures, that is, the entire human race, to the royal treasury."[5]

In a Holy Saturday hymn, Saint Basil praises the cross and mocks hell in these poetic words:

Today hell groans and cries aloud:
"My power has been destroyed.
I accepted a mortal man as one of the dead;
yet I cannot keep Him prisoner,
and with Him I shall lose all those whom I ruled.
I held in my power the dead from all ages;
but see, He has raised them all."
Glory to your Cross, O Lord, and to Your Resurrection.[6]

It is evident that in the sermons and hymns of the early church, the cross and the resurrection are not two divergent and opposite episodes, but a single divine movement of salvation. They depicted Christ invading hell, not as a captive, but as a conqueror emptying hell of its captives. The patristic harrowing of hell theology is derived directly from the apostolic theology of the descent of Christ into the realm of the dead.

In his letter to the Ephesians the apostle Paul cites and interprets Psalm 68:18 in a theologically creative way.

Therefore it is said,

"When he ascended on high, he made captivity itself a captive; he gave gifts to his people."

(When it says, "He ascended," what does it mean but that he had also descended into the lower parts of the earth? He who descended is the same one who ascended far above all the heavens, so that he might fill all things.) (Eph 4:8-10)

According to patristic theological imagination, Hades made the fatal mistake of assuming that it had made Christ yet another prisoner in its realm of the dead. But Christ was no prisoner, he was an invading conqueror. In his descent to the dead Christ made the captives of death his spoils of war, leading them out of hell into heaven.

Ephrem the Syrian writes about it like this,

> [The Lord] in his turn vanquished death through his great cry when he had gone up on the cross. Whereas death was binding one person on the cross, all those who had been bound in Sheol were being delivered because of the chains of one person . . . his hands, which delivered us from the bonds of death, were transfixed by nails. . . . [Death] stole him, took him away and put him in a tomb while he was asleep, but, on waking and standing up, he stole the stealer. This is the cross which crucifies those who crucified [the Lord], and this is the captive who leads into captivity those who had led him into captivity.[7]

According to the early Christian theologians, the crucifixion of Jesus Christ was a Trojan horse delivered to the devil. Christ was the ransom paid to death that death should never have accepted, for in accepting the ransom of Christ it led to the demise of death and the redemption of all the captives of Hades.

A patristic theology of Christ descending triumphantly into death is derived not only from Paul, but also from the mysterious account found in 1 Peter recounting Christ descending into Hades and preaching to the departed spirits imprisoned there.

> For Christ also suffered for sins once for all, the righteous for the unrighteous, in order to bring you to God. He was put to death in the flesh but made alive in the spirit, in which also he went and made a proclamation to the spirits in prison, who in

former times did not obey, when God waited patiently in the days of Noah, during the building of the ark, in which a few, that is, eight lives, were saved through water. (1 Peter 3:18-20)

Maximus the Confessor, who in my mind is the most erudite of all the patristic theologians, comments on Christ preaching to the imprisoned spirits in Hades in *Questions-Answers to Thalassius*.

These people were punished not so much for their ignorance of God as for the offences they imposed on one another. It was to them, according to [Saint Peter] that the great message of salvation was preached when they were already damned as men in the flesh, that is, when they received, through life in the flesh, punishment for crimes against one another, so that they could live according to God by the spirit, that is, being in hell, they accepted the preaching of the knowledge of God, believing in the Saviour who descended into hell to save the dead. So, in order to understand [this] passage in [Holy Scripture] let us take it this way: the dead, damned in the human flesh, were preached to precisely for the purpose that they may live according to God by the spirit.[8]

Odes of Solomon, a marvelous second-century Syrian theopoetics on Christ preaching in hell and liberating the captives, is perhaps the best example of the kind of atonement language most commonly employed by the early church. It recounts how salvation came to those imprisoned in Hades through Christ triumphantly shattering the gates of Sheol and sickening death with his entrance. Then it tells of how Christ formed a congregation of those held captive by death who ran to him begging for mercy and liberation.

May we also be saved with you, because you are our Savior.
Then I heard their voice, and placed their faith in my heart.
And I placed my name upon their head,
because they are free and they are mine.[9]

It is crucial to note that early Christian theology never spoke of the resurrection as merely a personal victory of Christ over death. Rather it spoke of the resurrection as a *cosmic victory*.

The whole point of Christ descending into death was to rescue those held captive by death. Saint Ambrose stressed this in the funeral sermon he preached for his brother, in which he said, "If Christ did not rise for us, then he did not rise at all, since he had no need of it just for himself. In him the world arose, in him heaven arose, in him the earth arose."[10] Christ died to raise the world.

Renowned New Testament scholar John Dominic Crossan has persuasively argued that Romans 1:4 should be translated and understood as saying that Jesus "was declared to be Son of God with power according to the spirit of holiness *by Christ's resurrection of the dead ones.*"[11] The patristic consensus regarding Christ's descent into Hades was that in his resurrection he raised the entire population of "dead ones" out of hell.

Commenting on this consensus, patristic scholar and Orthodox Metropolitan Hilarion Alfeyev says,

> It is clear that in the first four Christian centuries there was a significant degree of common understanding of this doctrine by theologians of the East and West. In particular, many Western authors shared the opinion of the Eastern fathers that all people, not only some, were saved by Christ when he descended into hell.[12]

For years now I have incorporated an Orthodox *Anastasis* (Resurrection) icon into my Easter sermon. In ancient Christian iconography, the resurrection is not depicted by Jesus as a lone individual departing the tomb of Joseph of Arimathea, but by his harrowing of hell. The *Anastasis* icon depicts both Christ's descent into death and his resurrection from the dead. This double movement is indicated in the fluttering robes of Christ. In the icon we see that Christ has descended into the black abyss of Hades. The gates of hell have fallen beneath the feet of Christ in the form of a cross, testifying to the truth that Christ defeated death by his own death upon the cross.

Scattered around the cross-shaped gates of hell are broken locks and chains. That Christ shattered the bars of hell was a common patristic theme. Saint Epiphanius, the fourth-century bishop of Cyprus, writing about Christ's descent into Hades says,

> His body was truly buried and for three days remained without soul, breathless, motionless; it was wrapped in a shroud, put in a grave, covered by a stone and sealed. His divinity, however, was neither sealed nor buried. Together with his holy soul it descended into the nether world and liberated captive souls from there; it destroyed the sting of death, demolished bars and locks of steel.[13]

Often in an *Anastasis* icon, death is personified as a bound and trampled-upon demon. Surrounding Christ is a burst of gold and blue light, indicating that Christ now fills heaven and hell with his presence.

As Paul says, "The same one who descended is the one who ascended higher than all the heavens, so that he might fill the entire universe with himself" (Eph 4:10 NLT). Christ is never depicted alone in an *Anastasis* icon. He is surrounded by a host of departed saints in Sheol awaiting their liberation—a host that always includes David, Solomon, and John the Baptist. The most exciting and instructive aspect of the icon is what Christ is doing. He is taking hold of an old man and an old woman and pulling them up out of their graves. Christ has taken hold of them by their wrists, indicating that they are not pulling themselves up out of death, but Christ alone is raising them. Who is this old couple? Of course, it's Adam and Eve. In their Hebrew origins, "Adam" means mankind, while "Eve" means living. Thus the icon portrays Christ saving living humankind from the dominion of death. I love everything about the ancient *Anastasis* icon!

Men in Black

But perhaps I can communicate the ancient patristic understanding of how Christ destroyed death by death using a more contemporary allegory. John Chrysostom compared the death and resurrection of Christ to Jonah being swallowed and then vomited by the whale. I'll compare the harrowing of hell to a moment in *Men in Black*. Yes, the 1997 science-fiction comedy starring Tommy Lee Jones and Will Smith. In the climactic scene of the film, Agent K (Tommy Lee Jones) goads a giant alien "galactic cockroach" known as a "bug" by shouting at it, "Eat me!" The bug, provoked by Agent K's incessant taunts, swallows him in a single, hideous gulp, and movie-viewers assume that the agent has perished. But in the belly of the bug, Agent K retrieves the weapon that has already been devoured and destroys the alien from inside. The evil alien's demise was achieved by a weapon deployed within "the belly of hell."

It's a modern Hollywood depiction of how the ancient church fathers thought of Christ as the ransom that first tricked and then destroyed death from the inside. When death dared to swallow the humanity of Christ, it was subsequently destroyed from within by the divinity of Christ. And, yes, I have shown this scene from *Men in Black* in our church on an Easter Sunday. That may strike some as introducing too much frivolity into the grandeur of Easter, but I think Chrysostom would approve.

Through his crucifixion, his descent into hell, his resurrection from the dead, and his ascension into the heavens, Christ now fills all things everywhere with himself. In his hymn of the cross, Paul speaks of Jesus' obedience to death, even death on a cross, resulting in his lordship extending to all who are in heaven, on earth, and under the earth.

> Therefore God exalted him even more highly
> and gave him the name
> that is above every other name,

so that at the name given to Jesus
   every knee should bend,
      in heaven and on earth and under the earth,
and every tongue should confess
   that Jesus Christ is Lord,
      to the glory of God the Father. (Phil 2:9-11)

In his harrowing of hell, Christ has filled even death with his saving presence. Truly it can be said, "If I make my bed in hell, behold, You are there" (Ps 139:8 NKJV). Today, for a human being to enter into death is not to encounter death, but to encounter Christ—to encounter him as both judge and savior. "Do not be afraid; I am the First and the Last. I am he who lives, and was dead, and behold, I am alive forevermore. Amen. And I have the keys of Hades and of Death" (Rev 1:17-18 NKJV).

18

THE LAMB UPON
THE THRONE

When the slaughtered Lamb is seen "in the midst" of the divine throne in heaven, the meaning is that Christ's sacrificial death belongs to the way God rules the world.

RICHARD BAUCKHAM,
THE THEOLOGY OF THE BOOK OF REVELATION

THE CRUCIFIXION OF JESUS CHRIST was the true coronation of the King of kings. His crown was a thorny one and his throne was the tree upon which he hung. When the Zebedee brothers James and John asked Jesus, "Appoint us to sit, one at your right hand and one at your left, in your glory" (Mk 10:37), they were unwittingly asking to be crucified with Jesus. This is why Jesus tells them, "You do not know what you are asking" (Mk 10:38). When James and John persisted in saying they were prepared to do whatever was necessary to be granted this honor, Jesus told them, "To sit at my right hand or at my left is not mine to appoint, but it is for those for whom it has been prepared" (Mk 10:40). It wasn't James and John who were at the right and left of Jesus in his glory, but the two thieves.

Christ crucified is Christ glorified. The cross was not shame; it was and is glory. It was not defeat; it was and is victory. It was not failure: it was and is the salvation of the world. Jesus Christ not only saves the world through the cross, he also rules the world from the cross. The kingdom that Christ established through his cross comes without any wars, without any battlefields, without any killing of enemies. Whatever justifies violence as a necessary means to a legitimate end is never the kingdom of heaven—it's only the latest iteration of Babylon. As citizens of the kingdom of heaven we persuade by love, witness, reason, rhetoric, Spirit, and if need be, martyrdom, but never by violence. Our king is Jesus Christ hung upon a tree, not Julius Caesar crossing the Rubicon. Our king wins his kingdom by dying, not by killing, by a sacrificial death, not a bloody conquest.

Yet if we are not vigilant in our theology, we can be tempted to leave the cross of Christ in the historical past and reduce it to a mere factor in an academic atonement equation. We are tempted to make the cross something we can be done with. If we make this mistake, we are prone to resort back to the myth of redemptive violence as the only real means of salvation. Atonement theories that limit the efficacy of the cross to the afterlife lead to perversities in theology. *Jesus with his cross saves my soul for heaven, but it's a good guy with a gun who will save the world.* I wish this line of thinking was a rare and bizarre oddity, but alas, I know from experience that it is distressingly common. For too many conservative American Christians the gun is as sacrosanct as the cross, and the Second Amendment is as revered as the Second Commandment.

The privileging of violence as the means by which the world will ultimately be saved is often given supposed biblical warrant through a misreading of the book of Revelation where the violent images are literalized. If the violence of Revelation is literal, then in the end God literally saves the world with violence—not a violence endured, but a violence inflicted. This distorts Christ into a conqueror who is not all that different from Genghis Khan. A misreading of the Apocalypse gives us an eschatology that poisons the whole gospel story. We end up with the Jesus of the Sermon on the Mount repudiating his own teaching as he slays his enemies by the millions. Christ crucified is abandoned for the pagan vision of a warrior god.

A trite but popular maxim says, "He came the first time as a lamb, but he's coming back as a lion." The idea is that the violence Jesus always eschewed during his life, he will eventually embrace at his second coming. As if the one who taught love of enemy and turning the other cheek will ultimately morph into Shiva the Destroyer, wreaking bloody carnage upon the world. Instead of "Jesus Christ is the same yesterday and today and forever" (Heb 13:8), it becomes "Jesus Christ is the same yesterday and today but look out for tomorrow!" This is what happens if we derive an eschatology from Revelation that envisions Christ as a literal apocalyptic warrior. So in our conversation about the cross we now need to look at how the cross is depicted in that strange and mysterious book at the end of the Bible.

THE BOOK OF REVELATION

The book of Revelation is a dizzying creative work in the genre of Jewish apocalyptic literature that concludes the New Testament canon. We have virtually no historic information on the author, John of Patmos, but we can surmise that he was probably an itinerant prophet familiar with the churches in the eastern provinces of the Roman Empire, and he may have been connected with the Johannine community in Ephesus. From the fantastical book he left us, I think of John the Revelator as an eccentric genius, the mad scientist of New Testament writers.

Above all, Revelation is a prophetic book, not so much in predicting the future, but in providing a transcendent perspective on Jesus Christ, the Roman Empire, and the course of history. Most of Revelation (chapters 6–18) gives a prophetic interpretation of the tumultuous events of the AD 60s and 70s and is especially concerned with interpreting the First Jewish War and the destruction of

Jerusalem in AD 70. Though the book was probably written during the reign of Domitian, it is set during the reign of Emperor Galba, the successor of that beastly persecutor of Christians, Emperor Nero—the numerical number of whose name is 666.

John fixes the historical setting of his Apocalypse not at the beginning of the book, but near the end in chapter seventeen: "This calls for a mind that has wisdom: the seven heads are seven mountains on which the woman is seated; also, they are seven kings, of whom five have fallen, one is living, and the other has not yet come, and when he comes, he must remain only a little while" (Rev 17:9-10). Rome was the city set on seven hills. The five fallen kings were the first five Caesars of imperial Rome: Augustus, Tiberius, Caligula, Claudius, and Nero. The one who "is living" was Emperor Galba, who reigned for seven months, and the seventh king who "remains only a little while" was Emperor Otho who only reigned for three months. Thus Revelation, composed around AD 95, is written from the perspective of someone living during the second half of AD 68.

Throughout the book, John unleashes a withering prophetic critique of the Roman Empire. For the Revelator, Rome is not the eternal city, but a demonic and doomed monstrosity. The beast, the false prophet, and the harlot are all symbols of Rome and Caesar controlled by the satanic dragon. John, the itinerant prophet, is deeply concerned with ensuring the seven churches of Asia are not seduced by the cult of the emperor that was on the rise in the eastern provinces. For him, there could be no conflation of Christ with imperial aspirations. Revelation remains powerfully relevant in its unsparing condemnation of civil religion and religious nationalism.

The book is at its most glorious in depicting the ultimate triumph of Christ and his kingdom. This is where Revelation is truly predictive. In remarkable ways John foresees the eventual triumph of Christ over the Roman Empire. In the final two chapters, he describes the kingdom of Christ as a city having the same dimensions as the Roman Empire as it descends from heaven (Rev 21:16). John foresees a future where the kingdom of Christ will replace the kingdom of Caesar. But the city is also fifteen hundred miles *high*, signifying that the kingdom of Christ unites heaven and earth. The coming of new Jerusalem is the answer to our constant prayer that God's will be done on earth as it is in heaven.

Revelation overflows with fantastic images in stylized hyperbole spanning the spectrum from the beautiful and glorious to the grotesque and hideous. In the pages of the Apocalypse we encounter bejeweled cities, smoking abysses, rivers of blood, lakes of fire, angelic creatures in heaven, and monstrous beasts rising from the sea. John is providing a cavalcade of prophetic images to counter the omnipresent propaganda seen in imperial statues, temples, inscriptions, and architecture. With these alternative images, John hopes to provide his readers with an alternative religious imagination.

Of course, all these images are *symbolic*—none of them are to be literalized. We are no more to expect a literal two-hundred-mile river of blood as high as a horse's bridle than we are to expect a literal seven-headed sea monster wearing ten crowns to rise out of the Mediterranean. Any interpretation that literalizes the metaphors of Revelation, especially violent metaphors, should disqualify that interpretation for any serious consideration. A kind of suspension-of-disbelief-playfulness is necessary to enter into the spirit of the Apocalypse. With this in mind, let's look at the central symbol of Revelation: the Lamb of God.

Jesus Christ is referred to as the Lamb twenty-eight times in Revelation. And this is no accidental number. John is obsessed with numbers and uses each number to communicate something specific. Fours and sevens are especially important in Revelation. John references the Lamb twenty-eight times, that is seven times four, because a major theme in his Apocalypse is that the divine Lamb (with his seven eyes and seven horns) reigns over the four corners of the earth.

The first time John introduces the Lamb is very significant. It occurs in the fifth chapter. The first chapter of the Apocalypse establishes that this book is a revelation of Jesus Christ given to a prophet named John while he was on the island of Patmos. Chapters two and three contain prophetic letters to seven churches in the Anatolian provinces of the Roman Empire—in what today is western Turkey. In chapter four, John presents his readers with a scene of heavenly worship around the throne of God. Chapter five gives us the high drama of the scroll and the Lamb.

REVELATION AS A GRECO-ROMAN PLAY

Though Revelation properly belongs to the genre of Jewish apocalyptic literature, some of Revelation is presented in the form of a Greco-Roman play, complete with drama, tragedy, comedy, and chorus. At times John of Patmos appears to be a playwright who imagines his production presented with elaborate sets, costumes, and choruses. In chapter five, we see all four elements of drama, tragedy, comedy, and chorus in succession.

The scene opens with the one seated upon the throne holding a scroll sealed with seven seals. As we will eventually discover, the scroll contains the divine declaration that brings about God's purpose for the world. The seven seals are not the *contents* of the scroll, but the *events* that precede its declaration. What is the declaration on the scroll? We discover this only after the seven seals have been broken and the seven trumpets have sounded.

> Then the seventh angel blew his trumpet, and there were loud voices in heaven, saying,
>
> > "The kingdom of the world has become the kingdom of
> > our Lord and of his Messiah,
> > and he will reign forever and ever." (Rev 11:15)

The opening of the scroll brings about the eternal reign of God on earth, yet only after one who is worthy has broken the seals.

But who is the worthy one? This is the drama, much like that of the later Arthurian legend of the Middle Ages. Who is the true king who can draw Excalibur from the stone? Who is the worthy one who can break the seals? Many can attempt to break the seals, but only the worthy one will succeed. A universal search for the worthy one is embarked upon, but then the drama becomes a tragedy. "And no one in heaven or on earth or under the earth was able to open the scroll or to look into it. And I began to weep bitterly because no one was found worthy to open the scroll or look into it" (Rev 5:3-4). What could be more tragic than to realize that our world is doomed to the futility of eternal recurrence, to an everlasting tyranny of futility?

But just when the tragedy seems unendurable, the plot takes an unexpected twist and turns into a comedy.

> Then one of the elders said to me, "Do not weep! See, the Lion of the tribe of Judah, the Root of David, has triumphed. He is able to open the scroll and its seven seals."
>
> Then I saw a Lamb, looking as if it had been slain, standing at the center of the throne. (Rev 5:5-6 NIV)

Do you see the comedy? The elder says, "Look! The Lion has triumphed!" But when John looks, he doesn't see a lion, he sees a little slaughtered lamb. That's comedy. There is no warring Lion in Revelation, only the Lamb. The Lamb is the divine joke played on the dragon and its beast.

The elder *refers* to the Lamb with the messianic titles because Jesus is the Messiah descended from the tribe of Judah and the royal line of David. But when John *looks*, he doesn't see a predatory lion, he sees a vulnerable Lamb, one that has been slain yet is somehow standing. What John sees is the slain and risen Lamb of God who is Jesus Christ. The beast has not yet appeared in John's Apocalypse, but when it does it will be presented in stark contrast. Just as Daniel's imperial beasts are eventually subdued by the Son of Man (see Daniel 7), so the beastly

Roman Empire and all its successors will be triumphed over by the slain Lamb. The dragon rules through the violent power of the beast, but God rules through the nonviolent, co-suffering love of the Lamb.

After the drama, tragedy, and comedy, we now have the chorus. The twenty-four elders begin to sing first, and then are joined by a vast choir of angels, until finally all creation joins in singing the anthem of the Lamb.

They sing a new song:

> "You are worthy to take the scroll
>   and to break its seals,
> for you were slaughtered and by your blood you ransomed
>   for God
>   saints from every tribe and language and people
>   and nation;
>   you have made them a kingdom and priests serving our God,
>   and they will reign on the earth."

Then I looked, and I heard the voice of many angels surrounding the throne and the living creatures and the elders; they numbered myriads of myriads and thousands of thousands, singing with full voice,

> "Worthy is the Lamb that was slaughtered
>   to receive power and wealth and wisdom and might
>   and honor and glory and blessing!"

Then I heard every creature in heaven and on earth and under the earth and in the sea, and all that is in them, singing,

> "To the one seated on the throne and to the Lamb
>   be blessing and honor and glory and might
> forever and ever!" (Rev 5:9-13)

When the slain Lamb is seen standing in the center of God's throne it combines two images that represent two theological themes: the sovereign rule of God and the sacrificial death of Christ. At the center of God's sovereignty is the sovereign choice to suffer. At the center of God's self-revelation is a slaughtered Lamb. The clearest revelation of who God is, is not seen in overawing displays of coercive power as with the pagan gods, but in Christ crucified.

If we imagine God as the omnipotent one seated upon a throne, we must always remember that at the center of this throne is the slaughtered Lamb. The sovereign throne and the suffering cross are not two different things—they are one and the same. The cross *is* the throne of God. The one upon the throne *is* the crucified one. The sacrificial death of Christ *is* the way that God rules the world. Christ does not rule with the thunderbolt of Zeus or the hammer of Thor. Christ always reigns from the cross, never from an F-16 fighter jet. If we literalize the metaphorical violence of Revelation, we create a theological catastrophe.

We end up with violence as God's salvific solution.

We end up with God saving the world by killing it.

We end up with God adopting the condemned way of Cain.

We end up with Jesus renouncing his Sermon on the Mount.

We end up with the cross of Christ as superfluous and even pointless.

We end up ruining the whole gospel story.

The Deeper Magic

In speaking of the sacrificial death of Christ, we must always remember that we are ransomed people *for* God, not *from* God. In like manner, an orthodox atonement theology understands that Christ does not save us *from* God, but *for* God. Thus the redeeming ransom is not paid *to* God, but *on behalf of* God. The ransom is paid to the abductor that held humanity captive: death and Hades. Jesus obtained the keys of death and Hades through his ransom. In the logic of ransom, the abductor does not pay himself the ransom.

As we saw in the previous chapter, the early church understood the ransom paid in Christ's blood as a kind of trick played on the devil, a Trojan horse trick that resulted in the liberation of humanity from the tyranny of death. It's the "deeper magic" of Aslan's sacrificial death in C. S. Lewis's *The Lion, the Witch and the Wardrobe*. When Aslan gave himself as a sacrificial ransom for Edmund, the White Witch was tricked. She not only lost Edmund, but all of Narnia.

Aslan explained it to Susan like this:

> Though the Witch knew the Deep Magic, there is a magic deeper still which she did not know. Her knowledge goes back only to the dawn of time. But if she could have looked a little further back, into the stillness and the darkness before Time dawned, she would have read there a different incantation. She would have known that when a willing victim who had committed no treachery was killed in a traitor's stead, the Table would crack and Death itself would start working backward.[1]

The first epistle of Peter also uses the language of lamb and ransom when it speaks of our redemption from futility. "You were ransomed from the futile conduct inherited from your ancestors, not with perishable things like silver or gold, but with the precious blood of Christ, like that of a lamb without defect or blemish" (1 Pet 1:18-19). The futility that Christ redeems us from is the "vanity of vanities" lamented by the Preacher in Ecclesiastes: Life rendered pointless and meaningless by the tyranny of death. The precious blood of Jesus rescues us from the yawning abyss of nihilism.

John the Revelator first introduces the Lamb in chapter five, and three times in that chapter he speaks of the Lamb as having been slaughtered. This is John's metaphorical language for Christ crucified. Every time John presents the Lamb in his Apocalypse, John intends for us to see a slaughtered Lamb. Throughout Revelation Christ is depicted as crucified and triumphant. The victorious Christ of Revelation does not reign despite his crucifixion, but through his crucifixion. Worthy is the Lamb!

19

THE CENTER
THAT HOLDS

Turning and turning in the widening gyre
The falcon cannot hear the falconer;
Things fall apart; the centre cannot hold.

W.B. YEATS, "THE SECOND COMING"

POETRY IS THE BEST VEHICLE we have for attempting to articulate the ineffable. This is why so much of the Bible is poetry. And not just the obvious poetry of the Psalms, the Writings, and the literary prophets in the Old Testament, but much of what we find in the New Testament as well. The Gospels and Epistles are far more poetic than we are accustomed to recognizing. And what is Revelation if not a phantasmic poem? The Bible is the product of a poetic age—the age of Homer and Isaiah, of Virgil and John the Revelator.

But we do not live in a poetic age. We live in a technical age, a digital age of 1s and 0s. We live in an age that Walter Brueggemann calls a "prose-flattened world."[1] The dominant language of our time languishes under the tyranny of prose. This has a quashing effect on our attempts to do creative theology. We don't want theopoetics. We want an owner's manual on God. We tell ourselves that prose is precise when it's mostly just unimaginative. A Spirit-inspired imagination is necessary for theological progress.

There is an open-endedness in poetry that allows for ongoing development and future interpretation. We see this time and again as the New Testament writers reinterpret the poems of the Hebrew prophets creatively in the light of Christ. Those who crave the fixedness of certitude tend to be frustrated by the fluidity of poetry. Where prose gets stuck in a cul-de-sac, poetry opens up to new vistas. What the Hebrew prophets saw they could only say in poetry. And what is true in the biblical text is true in the wider world. The poets are the seers. Sometimes they see what isn't and could be; sometimes they see vividly what the rest of the world is blind to.

THE SECOND COMING

William Butler Yeats was a seer-poet and perhaps the greatest of all the Irish poets. He was born near Dublin in 1865 and began writing poetry at seventeen. In 1923 he was awarded the Nobel Prize for Literature. Yeats's most famous poem is "The Second Coming," the first six lines of which adorn the back cover of my copy of a collection of his poems.

"The Second Coming" was written in 1919 in the aftermath of WWI, a catastrophe in Christendom born out of hubris and nationalism. With the emergence of mechanized and chemical weaponry, WWI resulted in the death of twenty million people. "The Second Coming" explores the world coming undone under the pressure of modern warfare. As the poet says, "Things fall apart; the centre cannot hold."[2] The poem envisions the world spinning out of control in an ever-expanding vortex of violence. It laments that humanity can no longer hear God—"The falcon cannot hear the falconer"—resulting in anarchy, the loss of innocence, and the "blood-dimmed tide" of war.

The poem yearns for the hope of the second coming of Christ but fears what will come instead is a pitiless monster imagined as the

Sphinx coming to life and threatening the whole world. The poem ends like this.

> The darkness drops again; but now I know
> That twenty centuries of stony sleep
> Were vexed to nightmare by a rocking cradle,
> And what rough beast, its hour come round at last,
> Slouches towards Bethlehem to be born?[3]

Yeats the poet becomes Yeats the prophet when he intuits a beast about to be born—not in Bethlehem but Berlin. He can be bleak in his portents, yet even the rise of the Third Reich cannot undo what Christ has accomplished.

In the last line of his poem "The Magi," Yeats describes Christ at Bethlehem as "The uncontrollable mystery on the bestial floor."[4] Language like this shows why we need poets. The uncontrollable mystery is as good a title for Christ as you'll hear from any theologian. I'm sure it's a title Saint Paul would readily embrace. So let's turn to Paul, who was far more of a poet than he's given credit for.

When he wasn't forced to do nitty-gritty pastoral work, like telling the Corinthians to refrain from suing one another and to stop getting drunk at the Lord's Supper, he could write quite poetically. Think of his famous ode to love that we know as 1 Corinthians 13. The opening line is as famous as any sonnet of Shakespeare. "Though I speak with the tongues of men and of angels, and have not charity, I am become as a sounding brass, or a tinkling cymbal" (1 Cor 13:1 KJV). Paul is at his best when he leans into theopoetics. One of the finest examples of this is found in the first chapter of Colossians where Paul contemplates the supremacy of Christ in splendid poetry. I've reproduced the passage below in verse form to assist an appreciation for the poetic nature of the text.

> He has rescued us from the power of darkness
> and transferred us into the kingdom of his beloved Son,

in whom we have redemption,
  the forgiveness of sins.
He is the image of the invisible God,
  the firstborn of all creation,
for in him *all things* in heaven and on earth were created,
  things visible and invisible,
  whether thrones or dominions or rulers or powers—
all things have been created through him and for him.
He himself is before *all things*,
  and in him *all things* hold together.
He is the head of the body, the church;
  he is the beginning, the firstborn from the dead,
  so that he might come to have first place in *all things*.[5]
For in him all the fullness of God was pleased to dwell,
  and through him God was pleased to reconcile to himself
    all things,
  whether on earth or in heaven,
  by making peace through the blood of his cross. (Col 1:13-20
    emphasis added)

In a scant eight verses Paul gives us no less than a dozen stunning christological diamonds.

Christ is the fullness of God.

Christ is the image of the invisible God.

Christ is the creator of all things.

Christ is the firstborn over all creation.

Christ is the firstborn from the dead.

Christ is before all things.

Christ is the one for whom are all things.

Christ has first place in all things.

Christ has redeemed and forgiven us.

Christ is the head of the church.

Christ has reconciled all things to himself.

Christ holds all things together.

Paul's poem ends with a universal shalom accomplished through the cross. The eschatological hope for the restoration of all things is found in the christological confession that all things have been created *through* and *for* Christ. The higher our Christology the greater our hope for *apokatastasis*—the "universal restoration" spoken of by Peter (Acts 3:21). Christ is the origin and telos of all creation. At the end of the epic saga of salvation told in the biblical story, Jesus Christ says, "I am the Alpha and the Omega, the First and the Last, the Beginning and the End" (Rev 22:13). Christ accomplishes this redemption from dissolution through the blood of his cross.

But we live between the worlds—the world that is and the world to come. It's true, as Yeats says, things *do* fall apart and there are centers that *cannot* hold. Anarchy and blood-dimmed tides *are* loosed upon the world. But it's also true that they will not have the final word for our world, for by the blood of his cross Christ redeems all things.

In its own way, Yeats's "Second Coming" was and is prophetically true. Rough beasts of nonbeing do indeed slouch toward their own Bethlehem to be born. Yeats saw the slouching rough beast of his day as clearly as the Revelator saw the blasphemous seven-headed beast rise from the sea. Yeats foresaw that the horror that had spread across Europe in the form of trench warfare and mustard gas was not the end of things falling apart, but the beginning. The First World War was not the "war to end all wars" as the naive optimists had imagined; it was but a grim prelude for something even worse. The rough beast being born would build Auschwitz and Buchenwald. Yeats wasn't wrong. But along with his rough beast, we must also remember his uncontrollable mystery, the one who condescends to be born on the bestial floor.

This is what Paul is reaching for in his poem, the heights of christological revelation we must ascend lest we despair for the world. And we who confess that Jesus Christ is the Savior of the world have no business despairing. We can be clear-eyed realists about the centers that do not hold, but at the same time we have a transcendent hope because of the one who through his cross holds all things together.

At Word of Life, the church I pastor in St. Joseph, Missouri, we have seven modern icons created by Ukrainian artist and iconographer Ivanka Demchuk. She belongs to a school of young artists in Lviv, Ukraine, who are creating modern icons that retain their traditional theological symbolism while pushing beyond the archaic Byzantine style of art. One of my favorites is her *Resurrection* icon—a modern take on the traditional *Anastasis*. The icon is typical of Demchuk's style—spartan lines in stark white, highlighted with blue and gold. In the icon Christ is seen liberating the dead out of Hades. Like the traditional *Anastasis* icon, the gates of hell have fallen beneath the feet of Christ in the form of a cross, but unlike Byzantine icons there are an equal number of women and men being liberated.

Obviously, this is both an artistic and theological improvement. As in the traditional icon, Christ is raising Adam and Eve, but Demchuk has depicted our first parents as considerably younger. With a keen eye and a bit of theological imagination you can perceive that Christ is spanning three worlds. At the bottom is the gray world of death where the cross has shattered the gates of hell. Surrounding Christ is a tawny rim upon which he has placed one foot—the world in which humankind is formed from the dust of the earth. Behind and around Christ is the deep blue world of the heavens, dotted with what could be stars or galaxies.

Paul tells us that Christ is the creator of all things. Astronomers now tell us that this creation contains at least 100 billion galaxies comprised of 200 billion trillion stars! This creation of our incomprehensibly vast cosmos began to come into being 13.8 billion years ago when the Logos said, "Let there be." In the fullness of time the Creator entered creation through the womb of a virgin, died upon a tree, and opened a door to the world to come.

When I look at Demchuk's *Resurrection* icon I see all of this. I see in art what Paul describes in poetry: "In him all things hold together"

(Col 1:17). The icon shows that Christ reconciles "to himself all things, whether on earth or in heaven, by making peace through the blood of his cross" (Col 1:20). Christ is the center that holds.

In Adam, death is the concluding terminus. Things fall apart. The center cannot hold. With death comes decay and decomposition, the final dissolution. The mortal children of men cannot escape their undoing by death. Left on our own, everything is inexorably drawn toward disorder. This is the third law of thermodynamics written as our epitaph. But this is precisely why the gospel is good news! "For as all die in Adam, so all will be made alive in Christ" (1 Cor 15:22). Only the Creator has the capacity to undo death and hold creation together. Christ did not create the cosmos only to withdraw from it. This is the dreary theology of eighteenth-century Deism with its absent clockmaker. Christian theology says that the Creator Christ is forever bound to the cosmos through his incarnation, one that is entirely salvific. The cosmos cannot help but be saved because Christ is the Savior of the cosmos.

Paul's language says that Christ holds all things together. The writer of Hebrews describes it like this: "He sustains all things by his powerful word" (Heb 1:3). Every star, every galaxy, every blade of grass, and every grain of sand is sustained by the word of Christ. Every created thing will reach its final telos because it is created by and for Christ. Christ does not create superfluously or futilely. Creation will become what Christ created it for. With mystical insight we can see at the center of the cosmos a hundred billion galaxies spiraling around their Creator who from a tree stretches out his arms to hold the cosmos together. These are the dazzling truths that mesmerize us as we climb the mountain of God and breathe the rarefied air of Paul's high Christology.

WHAT IS HELL?

But now let's climb down from these lofty peaks into the temperate valleys below and consider these mysteries in the context of our day-to-day lives, because when things fall apart, we need a center that holds. In *The Great Divorce*, a theological fantasy novel on heaven and hell, C.S. Lewis imagines hell as a gray, dreary town where the inhabitants are eventually separated from one another by vast distances because they cannot overcome their alienation toward one another. Is it true that, given enough time, only within the love of Christ can we be held together? I believe so. In a temporal world of entropy where things fall apart, what never ends? "Love never ends" (1 Cor 13:8).

In *No Exit*, an existentialist play by French philosopher Jean-Paul Sartre, three damned souls are locked in the same room in hell. But hell is not as they imagined it would be. It's just three people placed in the same room. Near the end of the play, Garcin, one of the damned, observes, "So this is hell. I'd never have believed it. You remember all we were told about the torture-chambers, the fire and brimstone, the 'burning marl.' Old wives' tales! There's no need for red-hot pokers. Hell is—other people!"[6]

There is truth here, but Sartre is only half right in claiming hell is other people. Dostoevsky tells the full truth when in *The Brothers Karamazov* Elder Zosima says, "I ask myself: 'What is hell?' And I answer thus: 'The sufferings of being no longer able to love.'"[7] Hell is not other people; hell is being unable to *love* other people. We can go the way of Garcin and find hell anywhere. Or we can go the way of Zosima and find heaven everywhere. Christ at the center is what makes the difference.

Our lives need an organizing center with sufficient spiritual gravity so we can "keep it together." Family and friends, careers and causes, hobbies and interests are all good things that pertain to our humanity, but in and of themselves they lack sufficient spiritual gravity to keep us properly centered. Christ alone is the center that holds. When the center is Christ, many good things find their proper place and enrich our lives, but Christ alone is qualified to occupy the sacred center. Anything else placed at the center of our lives becomes an idol . . . and idols always fall apart.

In 1 Samuel 5 is the comical story of the Philistines capturing the ark of the covenant and placing it in the temple of Dagon at Ashdod. The morning after, the Philistine priests discovered that Dagon had "fallen on his face to the ground before the ark of the LORD" (1 Sam 5:3). This was Dagon's "I've fallen and I can't get up" moment. The priests, no doubt rather sheepishly, helped the idol up and put it back in its place. But who needs a teetering god dependent upon human help?

Idols are sustained by their worshipers. Christ sustains all things by the word of his power. The next morning Dagon had again fallen, but this time he had gone to pieces. "Dagon had fallen on his face to the ground before the ark of the LORD, and the head of Dagon and both his hands were lying cut off upon the threshold" (1 Sam 5:4). When your idols fall apart, your life goes to pieces . . . and like Dagon, idols always fall apart.

Idols are controllable and predictable, but they are doomed to fall apart, and with their doom comes the disintegration of all that has been arranged around them. Christ, though, is no idol. He is the uncontrollable mystery. Christ in his humility condescended to be the uncontrollable mystery born on the bestial floor of Bethlehem's stable that the Creator might enter creation as a creature. The Creator fully participated in the struggles and toils of all who are called human. While still in his infancy, the Creator became a refugee as his family fled to Egypt to escape a cruel despot. In youth and young manhood, the Creator became a carpenter working rough-hewn timber with calloused hands. On Good Friday the calloused hands of the Creator-carpenter were nailed to rough-hewn timber and the tree of Calvary became the center of the cosmos—the center that holds, the center that heals, the center that inaugurates the world to come.

The tree of Calvary is the wood between the worlds.

A THEOPOETICS OF THE CROSS

THE WORLD ON THE FAR SIDE OF THE WOOD

And God said,
Let the dry land appear.
And it was so.
And God saw that it was good.
Then God said,
Let the earth bring forth
Trees of every kind.
And it was so.
And God saw that it was good.
And there was evening,
And there was morning,
The third day.

Three trillion trees.
They tell me that's how many trees there are these days,
though I imagine there was a time when there were many
more, before

the "cortege rhythm of falling timber."
God made trees on the third day.
On the third day—our ears perk up.
It's a green day—a day of loam soil and growing things.
A day so good that God saw it so, not once but twice.
An auspicious day—a good day to get married,
a wedding day—a day to turn water to wine.
On the third day God made trees of every kind.
Silver Birch and Blue Spruce,
Weeping Willow and Giant Sequoia,
Oak and Pine,
Apple and Orange,
Buckeye trees and Cypress trees,
the Banyan tree for Buddha to sit under,
a deciduous tree called Chinese Wonder,
the Sycamore who is a friend of mine,
the Thorny Locust who is not so kind,
and in the middle of the Garden was one of a kind,
the tree of life with the fruit of immortality.
When Adam and Eve were banished from Eden
for eating the forbidden fruit,
the tree was guarded by a fearsome angel
with a flaming sword turning every way.
But why?
I think it had to do with not getting stuck in the wrong kind
    of immortality.

I had a dream once. I dreamed I was giving a lecture at a college, and in the lecture hall there were four entities I was pointing to and talking about: a rock, a plant, a cat, a person. I said, "These four have four kinds of being. The rock has being but nothing more. The plant has being and life. The cat has being, life, and awareness. The person has being, life, awareness, and the self-awareness we call consciousness. The capacity for self-awareness is also the capacity for God-awareness, but it comes at the price of death-awareness. For in the day that you eat of it you shall surely die." The dream was true, but I think I woke up too soon.

To be a God-aware person is not the final development. We are called not only to know God, but to become like God. "Let us make man in our image, according to our likeness," said Elohim. "You are gods," wrote the psalmist. "You are gods," affirmed Jesus. "God became man that man might become god," insisted Athanasius. Theosis is our telos—the participation in the divine nature. But we only get there through death. As yet we're but a seed, a caterpillar, a babe in the womb waiting to be born. Beloved, now we are the offspring of God, but it has not yet appeared what we shall be. This world is but a womb. More on that anon.

Three trillion trees.
Trees for firewood and lumber,
   for warmth and shelter.
Fruit trees and olive trees,
   for delectable food and luxurious oil.
Hardwood oak, walnut, and mahogany,
   for crafting the necessary items of living . . .
And killing.
A club, a gallows, a cross. Of course
A CROSS.
Plato said that at the center of the soul of the cosmos there is
   a cross.
Plato *would* say something like that, proto-Christian that
   he was.
David foresaw much,
   when he spoke of a forsaken one with pierced hands,
   as they gambled for his clothes.
But Plato may have foreseen even more,
   when he spoke of a just one tortured and spat upon,
   and last of all crucified. Crucified by being

nailed to a tree—a tree of death that became the tree of life.
The tree that appears at the beginning of the Bible in the
    middle of the garden,
And then reappears at the end of the Bible in the middle of
    the garden city.
The Revelator called it the tree of life.
A clever scribe called it the tree of the Lamb.
And you know what? They're both right.
Three trillion trees and one became the wood between
    the worlds.
God died upon a tree
that by God's own death
a door might be opened to the world on the far side of
    the wood.
This world is a womb—a womb for the world to come.
This is a chrysalis cosmos still cocooned
    awaiting metamorphosis.
I once caught a glimpse of the "new world unfurled."

I had another dream. I dreamed I was in a big and beautiful city—I think it may have been Barcelona. The cityscape spread before my eyes. I saw tall buildings and wide boulevards. I saw shops and restaurants. I saw people sitting in parks and strolling along sidewalks. It was good and it all seemed very real. Then there were sirens. (In the Bible it's trumpets, but in my dream it was sirens.) Loud sirens! Everyone knew what the sirens meant. It was kingdom come! Some were exultant, some were afraid—but whether happy or frightened it was kingdom come for each and everyone.

And as I looked, the cityscape before my eyes—which had seemed so real, so substantial—began to flutter, and then it began to tear, as if it were made of mere fabric. And as the fabric of the cityscape began to tear away, there appeared a new city, a new Barcelona, if you will. The new city was not entirely different, for there was a continuity with the old city, but the new city was far more glorious, far more dazzling, far more beautiful, and far more substantial. *For here we have no enduring city, but there is an eternal city to come. I saw the holy city coming down from heaven adorned as a bride for her husband.* That heavenly city which is to come is the world on the far side of the wood.

Three trillion trees.
They came to be on the third day of Creation.
That double-blessed day of verdant goodness.
Three trillion trees.
One became the wood upon which the Son of God was hung.
A tree created on the third day.
The third day—the day of three trillion trees.
And on the third day of new creation
the stone was rolled away.
On the third day the gardener walked again in the garden.
On the third day the firstborn emerged from a cocoon
       called death.
On the third day a new world was born.
There is the world that was and the world to come,
and between those two worlds
is the wood upon which the Son of God was hung.
Three trillion trees.
One became the wood between the worlds.

ACKNOWLEDGMENTS

PERI ZAHND IS MY WIFE, best friend, fellow adventurer, and copastor. She is also the first editor of all my books. Every writing day concludes with her reading my work back to me, making corrections, offering suggestions, and supplying other invaluable contributions. In my vanity I also like to think of her as my most enthusiastic reader. Thank you, Peri!

The Squad, to whom this book is affectionately dedicated, consists of my three amigos: Joseph Beach, Bradley Jersak, and Kenneth Tanner. They are my primary theological conversation partners, and there's no doubt I think better about our shared Christian faith because of them. Joe, Brad, Ken, keep on rockin' in the free world!

I would like to thank my literary agent, Andrea Heinecke, for always being in my corner, always being helpful and professional, and always being encouraging and supportive. Andrea makes my life as an author much easier.

Elissa Schauer was my editor for this book and for *When Everything's on Fire*. Elissa's intelligence, encouragement, and commitment to excellence make her a joy to work with, and she makes my work better. She has my appreciation and gratitude.

I extend my heartfelt appreciation to all the hardworking people at InterVarsity Press. The genuine passion they have for their good work is evident, and I am grateful.

To the staff at Word of Life Church I say thank you for being the best team I've ever worked with in forty-two years of ministry. Because of you I really do serve the Lord with gladness.

Finally, I want to thank Ivanka Demchuk for the gracious permission to reproduce her beautiful modern icon, *Resurrection,* in this book. Ivanka and her family live in Lviv, Ukraine, and I pray daily for peace to return to the land she calls home.

NOTES

PRELUDE

[1]Christian Smith, *The Bible Made Impossible* (Grand Rapids, MI: Brazos Press, 2011), x.

1. THE WOOD BETWEEN THE WORLDS

[1]Mother Julian of Norwich, *Revelations of Divine Love*, ed. Halcyon Backhouse and Rhona Pipe (London: Hodder & Stoughton, Ltd, 1987), 85.

[2]Walter Brueggemann, *Reality, Grief, Hope: Three Urgent Prophetic Tasks* (Grand Rapids, MI: Eerdmans, 2014).

[3]Fleming Rutledge, *The Crucifixion: Understanding the Death of Jesus Christ* (Grand Rapids, MI: Eerdmans, 2015), 75.

2. THE SINGULARITY OF GOOD FRIDAY

[1]I have also written on this elsewhere. See "The Singularity of Good Friday," Brian Zahnd, April 15, 2022, https://brianzahnd.com/2022/04/the-singularity-of-good -friday/.

[2]N. T. Wright, *The Day the Revolution Began: Reconsidering the Meaning of Jesus's Crucifixion* (New York: HarperOne, 2016), 74.

[3]Wright, *The Day the Revolution Began*, 43.

3. GOD REVEALED IN DEATH

[1]Joel C. Elowsky, ed., *Ancient Commentary on Scripture: New Testament IVb* (Downers Grove, IL: InterVarsity Press, 2007), 327.

4. GOD ON THE GALLOWS

[1]Fyodor Dostoevsky, *The Brothers Karamazov*, trans. Richard Pevear and Larissa Volokhonsky (San Francisco: North Point Press, 1990), 238.

[2]Dostoevsky, *Brothers Karamazov*, 242.

[3]Dostoevsky, *Brothers Karamazov*, 243.

[4]Dostoevsky, *Brothers Karamazov*, 245.

[5]Dostoevsky, *Brothers Karamazov*, 245.

[6]Dostoevsky, *Brothers Karamazov*, 318, 319, 320, 321, 322.

[7]Dostoevsky, *Brothers Karamazov*, 776.

[8]Elie Wiesel, *Night* (Norwalk, CT: The Easton Press, 2000), 56.

[9]Wiesel, *Night*, 91.

[10]Wiesel, *Night*, 92.

[11]Bruce Cockburn, "Dweller by a Dark Stream," by Bruce Cockburn, *Mummy Dust*, Golden Mountain Music Corp., 1981.

[12]Dietrich Bonhoeffer, *Letters and Papers from Prison* (New York: Touchstone, 1997), 361.

[13]Jürgen Moltmann, *The Crucified God* (Minneapolis: Fortress Press, 1993), 223.

[14]Moltmann, *Crucified God*, 278.

[15]Wiesel, *Night*, 154.

[16]Eugene H. Peterson, *The Jesus Way* (Grand Rapids, MI: Eerdmans, 2007), 158.

[17]Peterson, *Jesus Way*, 159.

5. THE ROAD OF DISCIPLESHIP

[1]Brian Zahnd, *Postcards from Babylon: The Church in American Exile* (St. Joseph, MO: Spello Press, 2019), i.

[2]Dietrich Bonhoeffer, *The Cost of Discipleship* (New York: Simon & Schuster, 1959), 89.

[3]Bonhoeffer, *Cost of Discipleship*, 88, 89.

[4]Bonhoeffer, *Cost of Discipleship*, 43.

[5]Bonhoeffer, *Cost of Discipleship*, 44, 45.

[6]Bonhoeffer, *Cost of Discipleship*, 89.

[7]Denver Catholic Staff, "Solitary, But Not Alone," *Denver Catholic*, March 28, 2016, https://denvercatholic.org/franz-jagerstatter-solitary-but-not-alone.

[8]*A Hidden Life*, directed and written by Terrence Malick (Century City, CA: Searchlight Pictures, 2019).

[9]Søren Kierkegaard, *Provocations: Spiritual Writings of Kierkegaard*, comp. and ed. Charles E. Moore (Maryknoll, NY: Orbis, 2003), 86.

[10]George Eliot, *Middlemarch* (New York: H. M. Caldwell Company, 1872), book 8, finale.

6. A LOVE SUPREME

[1]John Coltrane, "A Love Supreme," AlbumLinerNotes.com, accessed June 27, 2023, http://albumlinernotes.com/A_Love_Supreme.html.

[2]Cornel West, *Brother West: Living and Loving Out Loud* (New York: SmileyBooks, 2009), 6, 123.

[3]Hans Urs von Balthasar, *Love Alone Is Credible* (San Francisco: Ignatius Press, 2004), 84.

[4]Hans Urs von Balthasar and Adrienne von Speyr, *To the Heart of the Mystery of Redemption* (San Francisco: Ignatius Press, 2010), 73.

[5]Speyr, *Mystery of Redemption*, 73-74.

[6]Sergius Bulgakov, *The Lamb of God* (Grand Rapids, MI: Eerdmans, 2008), 353.

[7]Bulgakov, *The Lamb of God*, 371.

7. A GROTESQUE BEAUTY

[1]Judith Couchman, *The Mystery of the Cross* (Downers Grove, IL: InterVarsity Press, 2009), 88.

[2]Couchman, *Mystery of the Cross*, 88.

[3]Robert L. Wilken, *The Christians as the Romans Saw Them* (New Haven, CT: Yale University Press, 1984), 96.

[4]Couchman, *Mystery of the Cross*, 93.

[5]Marilyn Stokstad, *Medieval Art* (Boulder, CO: Westview Publishing, 2004), 180.

[6]Miguel de Cervantes, *Don Quixote* (New York: HarperCollins, 2003), 327.

[7]The Book of Common Prayer, 2006 General Convention (New York: Oxford University Press, 2007), 123.

8. What Is Truth?

[1]Frederick Buechner, *Telling the Truth: The Gospel as Tragedy, Comedy, and Fairy Tale* (San Francisco: HarperSanFrancisco, 1977), 13-14.

[2]Mikhail Bulgakov, *The Master and Margarita* (New York: Everyman's Library, 1992), 28.

[3]Bulgakov, *Master and Margarita*, 29-30.

[4]The NRSVUE says "Jews," but following the New Testament translations of David Bentley Hart and N. T. Wright, I prefer to render the word as "Judeans."

[5]"Friend of Caesar" is a technical term that refers to an ally of the emperor.

[6]Miroslav Volf, *Exclusion and Embrace* (Nashville: Abingdon Press, 1996), 276.

10. One Ring to Rule Them All

[1]Fleming Rutledge, *The Battle for Middle-earth: Tolkien's Divine Design in The Lord of the Rings* (Grand Rapids, MI: Eerdmans, 2004), 48.

[2]Rutledge, *Battle for Middle-earth*, 14.

[3]Lord Acton to Archbishop Mandell Creighton, April 5, 1887, https://history.hanover.edu/courses/excerpts/165acton.html.

[4]J. R. R. Tolkien, *The Fellowship of the Ring* (New York: Houghton Mifflin Company, 2002), 60.

[5]Tolkien, *Fellowship of the Ring*, 368.

[6]J. R. R. Tolkien, *The Return of the King* (New York: Houghton Mifflin Company, 2002), 911.

[7]Tolkien, *Fellowship of the Ring*, 260.

[8]Tolkien, *Fellowship of the Ring*, 260.

[9]Kristin Kobes Du Mez, *Jesus and John Wayne: How White Evangelicals Corrupted a Faith and Fractured a Nation* (New York: Liveright Publishing Corporation, 2020), 1.

[10]Elizabeth Diaz, "Christianity Will Have Power," *New York Times*, August 9, 2020, www.nytimes.com/2020/08/09/us/evangelicals-trump-christianity.html.

[11]Du Mez, *Jesus and John Wayne*, 1.

[12]Tolkien, *Fellowship of the Ring*, 401.

[13]Du Mez, *Jesus and John Wayne*, 14.

[14]Rutledge, *Battle for Middle-earth*, 180.

[15]Vatican News staff, "Pope to Russian Patriarch: 'Church uses language of Jesus, not of politics,'" *Vatican News*, March 16, 2022, www.vaticannews.va/en/pope/news/2022-03/pope-francis-calls-patriarch-kirill-orthodox-patriarch-ukraine.html.

[16]Jason Horowitz, "The Russian Orthodox Leader at the Core of Putin's Ambitions," *New York Times*, May 21, 2022, www.nytimes.com/2022/05/21/world/europe/kirill-putin-russian-orthodox-church.html.

[17]Peter Smith, "Moscow patriarch stokes Orthodox tensions with war remarks," *Associated Press*, March 8, 2022, https://apnews.com/article/russia-ukraine-putin-religion-europe-moscow-0670305be2e010e02a4e195ced2b7523.

[18]Tolkien, *The Return of the King*, 961.

[19]Tolkien, *The Return of the King*, 962-63.

11. WAR IS OVER (IF YOU WANT IT)

[1]Sergii Bulgakov, *The Apocalypse of John*, trans. Mike Whitton, revised by Michael Miller (Münster, Germany: Aschendorff Verlag, 2019), 157, 159.

12. THE SACRIFICE TO END SACRIFICING

[1]René Girard, *The Girard Reader*, ed. James G. Williams (New York: The Crossroads Publishing Company, 1996), 284-85.

[2]Girard, *Girard Reader*, 288.

[3]René Girard, *Sacrifice*, trans. Matthew Pattillo and David Dawson (East Lansing, MI: Michigan State University Press, 2011), 72.

[4]Girard, *Sacrifice*, xi.

[5]René Girard, *I See Satan Fall Like Lightning*, trans. by James G. Williams (Maryknoll, NY: Orbis Books, 2001), 191.

[6]Girard, *Girard Reader*, 186.

[7]Girard, *Girard Reader*, 183.

[8]Debbie Blue, *Consider the Women: A Provocative Guide to Three Matriarchs of the Bible* (Grand Rapids, MI: Eerdmans, 2019), 10.

[9]Girard, *Sacrifice*, 86.

13. THE LYNCHING OF THE SON OF MAN

[1]James H. Cone, *The Cross and the Lynching Tree* (Maryknoll, NY: Orbis Books, 2011), 1.

[2]René Girard, *The Girard Reader*, ed. by James G. Williams (New York: The Crossroads Publishing Company, 1996), 202.

[3]Neil Young, "Southern Man," by Neil Young, *After the Gold Rush*, Reprise, 1970.

[4]Cone, *Lynching Tree*, 158.

[5]Cone, *Lynching Tree*, 30.

[6]Cone, *Lynching Tree*, 31.

[7]Michelle Sanchez, "Bonhoeffer's Black Jesus," *Outreach Magazine*, September 14, 2020, https://outreachmagazine.com/features/leadership/58837-bonhoeffers-black-jesus.html.

[8]Robert Johnson, "Hell Hound on My Trail," by Robert Johnson, Vocalion, 1937.

[9] *Time* staff, "The Best of The Century," *Time*, December 31, 1999, https://content .time.com/time/subscriber/article/0,33009,993039-1,00.html.

[10] Billie Holiday, "Strange Fruit," by Abel Meeropol, Commodore, 1939.

[11] Cone, *Lynching Tree*, 138.

[12] Cone, *Lynching Tree*, 21-22.

[13] Cone, *Lynching Tree*, 160.

[14] Cone, *Lynching Tree*, 166.

14. The Cross and Capital Punishment

[1] Shane Claiborne, *Executing Grace* (New York: HarperOne, 2016), 54.

[2] Albert Mohler, "Why Christians Should Support the Death Penalty," *CNN Belief Blog*, May 1, 2014, https://religion.blogs.cnn.com/2014/05/01/why-christians-should -support-the-death-penalty.

[3] Claiborne, *Executing*, 140.

[4] Claiborne, *Executing*, 61.

[5] "Innocence Database," Death Penalty Information Center, accessed June 2, 2022, https://deathpenaltyinfo.org/policy-issues/innocence-database.

[6] Augustine, "Letter CXXXIII," *Nicene and Post-Nicene Fathers, Volume I*, ed. Philip Schaff (Peabody, MA: Hendrickson Publishers, 1994), 470.

[7] John Marshall, *John Locke, Toleration, and Early Enlightenment* (Cambridge: Cambridge University Press, 2010), 325.

[8] Pope Francis, "Fratelli Tutti," article 263, www.vatican.va/content/francesco/en /encyclicals/documents/papa-francesco_20201003_enciclica-fratelli-tutti.html.

15. The Sword-Pierced Soul of Mary

[1] "More Spacious than the Heavens," quoted in George Ryan, "The Best Obscure Marian Titles You Probably Don't Know," uCatholic, August 8, 2022, https:// ucatholic.com/blog/the-best-obscure-marian-titles-you-probably-dont-know/.

[2] Athanasius of Alexandria, *On the Incarnation* (CreateSpace Independent Publishing Platform, 2016), 24.

16. Three Trees on the Low Sky

[1] C. S. Lewis, *The Problem of Pain* (New York: Macmillan, 1962), 127.

[2] *Calvary*, directed by John Michael McDonagh (Galway, Ireland: Fís Éireann, 2014).

[3] George MacDonald, *Unspoken Sermons* (Whitehorn, CA: Johannsen, 1997), 64.

[4] C.S. Lewis, *George MacDonald: An Anthology* (San Francisco: HarperSanFrancisco, 2001), xxxvi.

17. The Harrowing of Hell

[1] Hilarion Alfeyev, *Christ the Conqueror of Hell: The Descent into Hades from an Orthodox Perspective* (Crestwood, NY: St. Vladimir's Seminary Press, 2009), 34.

[2] Alfeyev, *Christ the Conqueror*, 35-36.

[3] Alfeyev, *Christ the Conqueror*, 218, emphasis added.

[4] Alfeyev, *Christ the Conqueror*, 65-66.

[5] Alfeyev, *Christ the Conqueror*, 65.

[6] "Great and Holy Saturday: Great Vespers and Divine Liturgy of St. Basil the Great," Ukrainian Catholic Eparchy of Edmonton, https://eeparchy.com/liturgical -propers/great-lent-triodion/great-and-holy-saturday-great-vespers-and-divine -liturgy-of-st-basil-the-great.

[7] Alfeyev, *Christ the Conqueror*, 71.

[8] Alfeyev, *Christ the Conqueror*, 79.

[9] Alfeyev, *Christ the Conqueror*, 42.

[10] John Dominic Crossan and Sarah Sexton Crossan, *Resurrection Easter: How the West Lost and the East Kept the Original Easter Vision* (San Francisco: HarperOne, 2018), 1.

[11] Crossan, *Resurrection Easter*, 67. Emphasis added.

[12] Alfeyev, *Christ the Conqueror*, 100.

[13] Alfeyev, *Christ the Conqueror*, 68.

18. The Lamb upon the Throne

[1] C.S. Lewis, *The Lion, the Witch and the Wardrobe*, Chronicles of Narnia (New York: HarperTrophy, 1994), 125.

19. The Center That Holds

[1] Walter Brueggemann, *Finally Comes the Poet* (Minneapolis: Augsburg Press, 1989), 1.

[2] W.B. Yeats, "The Second Coming," *Poems Selected by Seamus Heaney* (London: Faber and Faber, 2000), 64.

[3] Yeats, "The Second Coming," 64.

[4] Yeats, "The Magi," *Poems Selected*, 42.

[5] The NRSVUE translates the end of verse 18 as "first place in *everything*." Nevertheless, it is the same word (*pas*) that is translated "all things" five other times in this passage. I have changed "everything" to "all things" to maintain Paul's refrain of "all things."

[6] Jean-Paul Sartre, *No Exit and Three Other Plays*, trans. by Stuart Gilbert (New York: Vintage International, 1989), 45.

[7] Fyodor Dostoevsky, *The Brothers Karamazov*, trans. Richard Pevear and Larissa Volokhonsky (San Francisco: North Point Press, 1990), 322.

IMAGE CREDITS

Alexamenos graffito, *Le Crucifix du Palatin* (anonymous reproduction), Roman graffiti scratched in a wall, ancient Rome, third century / public domain, Wikimedia Commons

Unknown, crucifix in Zabaldika, Navarre, Spain / photo by Brian Zahnd, used with permission

Matthias Grünewald, Nikolaus Hagenauer, *Isenheim Altarpiece* (1509–1515), Unterlinden Museum / public domain, Wikimedia Commons

Andreas Pavias, *The Crucifixion* (15th century), National Gallery of Athens / public domain, Wikimedia Commons

Hieronymus Bosch, *Christ Carrying the Cross* (1505–1507), Royal Monastery of San Lorenzo de El Escorial / public domain, Wikimedia Commons

Big Love, portion of mosaic in Golgotha chapel at the Church of the Holy Sepulchre in Jerusalem / photo by Peri Zahnd, used with permission

Sandro Botticelli, *Holy Trinity (Pala della Convertite)* (1491–1494), Courtauld Institute of Art / public domain, Wikimedia Commons

Andrea Mantegna, *Crucifixion* (1459), Louvre Museum / public domain, Wikimedia Commons

Unknown, cross icon / photo by Brian Zahnd, used with permission

Fra Angelico, *Saint Dominic Adoring the Crucifixion* / photo by Brian Zahnd, used with permission

Unknown, *Gero Crucifix*, circa 970, Cologne Cathedral / Pedelecs, Creative Commons license, Wikimedia Commons

Antonio Ciseri, *Ecce Homo* (1871), MASI Lugano museum / public domain, Wikimedia Commons

Frank Dicksee, *The Two Crowns* (1900), Tate Britain museum / public domain, Wikimedia Commons

Dormition Abbey fresco, Jerusalem / photo by Brian Zahnd, used with permission

Anastasis fresco, depicting the resurrection of Christ, Church of St. Savior in Chora, Istanbul / Jospeh Karnak, Creative Commons license, Wikimedia Commons

Ivanka Demchuk, *Resurrection* / used with permission

ALSO BY BRIAN ZAHND

When Everything's on Fire
978-1-5140-0333-6